SATAN'S SUBTERFUGE

Fred DeRuvo

STUDY · GROW · KNOW

www.studygrowknow.com

Published in Scotts Valley, California, by Study-Grow-Know
www.studygrowknow.com • www.rightly-dividing.com • www.adroitpublications.com

Scripture quotations unless otherwise noted, are from The Holy Bible, King James Version. This version is in the public domain.

Images used in this publication (unless otherwise noted) are from clipartconnection.com and used with permission, ©2007 JUPITERIMAGES, and its licensors. All rights reserved.

All Woodcuts used herein are in the Public Domain and free of copyright.

All Figure illustrations used in this book were created by the author and protected under copyright laws, © 2010.

Cover Design: Fred DeRuvo

Library of Congress Cataloging-in-Publication Data

DeRuvo, Fred, 1957 –

ISBN 0982644345
EAN-13 9780982644348

1. Religion – Christian Theology - Angelology & Demonology

Contents

Foreword: 5

Introduction: The Church 13

Chapter 1:   Child Abuse 19

Chapter 2:   Don't Like Yourself? 28

Chapter 3:   Blinded 38

Chapter 4:   Spiritual Mediocrity 45

Chapter 5:   On the Offense 48

Chapter 6:   Our State 52

Chapter 7:   The Greatest Commandment 69

Chapter 8:   Our Sin Nature... 87

Chapter 9:   Saved From...Saved To 94

Chapter 10: Abiding IN Christ.. 101

Chapter 11: Agony of Victory 127

Chapter 12: Fixing Our Eyes On Him 135

Chapter 13: Our Divine Riches: The Greatest Secret 144

Chapter 14: Pursuing Holiness 155

Resources for Further Study 169

"but ye are washed, but ye are sanctified, but ye are justified in the name of the Lord Jesus, and by the Spirit of our God."

– 1 Corinthians 6:11 (KJV)

FOREWORD

The subjects I deal with herein are difficult; *salvation*, the finished work of Christ, the believer's *standing* before God, and others of a similar nature. What I do *not* want to do is come across as someone who knows it all, someone who has *arrived* and no longer needs to study, or seek the Lord's will. This of course, is far from the truth.

I have certain beliefs, which I base upon God's Word, as we all do. The responsibility I have is to ensure that – to the best of my ability – what I teach, what I preach, what I write is *God's* meaning, not mine. I'm sure you would agree that this is why those of us who teach come under the greater condemnation, because we represent the very words of God. If we are wrong, then woe to us. That thought alone should be one that we ponder for quite some time before we ever put pen to paper, or voice to words.

I believe there are a number of problems within the *visible* Church today, as I'm sure you do as well. The problem though is that at least in some cases, the visible Church is confused by many with the *invisible* Church. People speak of the "fact" that the Church needs to be *purified*. They bemoan the fact that Christians are living lascivious lives, which bring dishonor to God. That may well be, however the Bride of Christ is pure, because no sin can touch Him.

I would agree that not all authentic Christians live their lives in such a way that God is glorified all the time. I would not agree that the *invisible* Church has somehow become *contaminated*. That, as far as I can see from Scripture, is *impossible*.

Consider the fact that Jesus Christ is *perfect*. He has *never* been sullied by sin of any kind. He never once gave into temptation, and never once needed to ask God the Father for forgiveness for Himself. It was unnecessary because Jesus Christ never did anything requiring God the Father to forgive Him.

When a person becomes a Christian, they are immediately baptized into Christ's Body. (We will get into the Scriptural particulars as we go through this book.) The Christian is not only baptized into His Body, but also the Holy Spirit takes up residence within us. Beyond this, we *are made* a new creation, being given a brand new spirit (God having "surgically" removed our old one). This new spirit within us can *never* sin (because it is hidden with Christ; cf. Ephesians 2), nor can it become corrupted by the sin nature which *remains* within us (though God has replaced our corrupt spirit with a new one. This sin nature remains with us until the day that we stand before Christ at the BEMA Judgment Seat.

If my *new spirit* cannot sin, and if my *new creation* is something that will never be contaminated in this life by any sin within me, and if that new spirit and new creation actually resides within Christ's Body, then how is it possible that His Body (the invisible Church) can somehow become corrupted or tainted? If that *could* occur, then this means that Christ Himself would be able to become corrupted and/or tainted. God forbid! This *cannot* occur. My sin *never* corrupts the *invisible* Church (Christ's Body). We will discuss what my sin (and yours) *does* do when it occurs, as I continue to live in this body of flesh.

I want you to know that I believe there is an extremely *insidious* attack on the authentic Christian today by the master deceiver himself. On the surface, it has every appearance of *piety* and *holiness*. The problem though is that I do not believe that it is *either*.

One of the chief ways in which Satan brings this attack on us is by making us *blind* to the truth of our *position* in Christ. We are often taught that the wiles of the devil include all manner of *assaults*, normally seen in *trials*, *tribulations*, and *persecutions*. These become obvious, leaving the believer with little doubt that they are being attacked by the enemy of their souls.

What we seem to *not* be aware of is the *spiritual knowledge* to which Satan *blinds us.* You may think that this is obvious, but judging from what is taught in many churches today, Christians seem completely unaware of the great truths revealed in God's Word.

I believe that the teachings of some churches largely focus on our *sin,* our *sin nature,* and our *corruption.* We are made to consider that we as believers must *feel* a certain way about ourselves. We are conditioned to adopt the attitude that makes us *want* to attack the things within us that make us sin. In fact, in some quarters, it is not good enough to hate our sin. We are taught to wallow in abject and thorough horror at all that we are, all that we do, and all that we feel, regarding *sin.* In other words, the authentic Christian is the depressed and often defeated Christian, who is so aware of his own sin that merely a glance at his sin puts him into fits of crying where nothing will pull them out of it. It is fashionable and expected for each Christian to come to be spiritually *broken.* In fact, other believers often view this behavior as *pious* as does that particular believer as well.

I do without equivocation *believe* that while sin *is* abhorrent, reprehensible, and the reason Christ died a sinless death, in which He took on God's wrath that was meant for *me,* God does *not* delight in watching us *berate* ourselves, *beat* ourselves up, or attempt to cultivate an attitude that *demeans* ourselves. In my opinion, this is a *false* sense of piety, an outward expression of religion *without* the power that winds up removing the joy of our salvation from our lives.

Why does God *not* want us to do this? For the simple reason that as believers, He does *not,* nor will *ever,* condemn us for any sin in our lives. All of our sin has already been judged on Calvary's cross. It can be no other way, and we will deal with this in detail.

I want to make it *extremely* clear that *never* are Christians to take a laissez-faire attitude when it comes to sin. Sin is *never* acceptable under any circumstances. We can never wink at it, think that God ignores it, or in any way minimize sin. Sin sent Jesus to the cross and it is sin that caused God, the Father's wrath to be poured out onto God, the Son. Sin causes death in all respects. The Christian can never, *ever* come to think that sin is excusable. It is not.

However, for the believer who believes that God is *impressed* with, or *desires* our outward (or even inward) displays of how much we hate sin, or attempts to work ourselves up into fits of emotions overflowing with hatred, anger, and abject remonstration of ourselves, let it be said that I do not find this in Scripture.

Is our sin *dealt* with – *past, present*, and *future* – or are we still *paying* for it? Could we have actually done something to eradicate our sin *prior* to becoming a believer and prior to Christ's death? If not, then why do we believe God is pleased for the emotional hoops that we jump through as we attempt to show Him how bad we feel about our sin? He does not condemn us now or ever, yet we often condemn ourselves.

Is salvation God's work, or is it something we must work with God to achieve? Most would agree that it is God's work, at least from the start. Others, while agreeing with this, would state that salvation is *maintained* by the Christian himself. I disagree strongly. While I agree that there is a human responsibility involved in salvation, it is God Himself who is the Author and Finisher of our salvation (cf. Hebrews 12:1-2).

However, *what exactly* is salvation and *how* is salvation *received*? For the longest time in evangelical circles, the idea that all one has to do is pray the "sinner's prayer" (come into my heart, etc.), and voila! salvation is gained. However, that is not biblical. It is impossible to find that in Scripture. Try it. Try to find any narrative that describes that happened when people received salvation and you will *not* find that they prayed any sinner's prayer, or raised their hand during a meeting with Paul, or Peter. They also did not "walk down the aisle" toward a new life.

Salvation is a *spiritual transaction.* It is God imparting life to me, a sinner. It is God destroying the Law's hold on me meritoriously. In other words, I am not beholden to the Law *for salvation*, which is something that the Law cannot give anyway. All the Law can do is point out my *faults, mistakes,* and *sin.* It has no ability to make me holy. It just tells me that I am *not* holy because I sin.

Most of us can turn to John 3, where Jesus is discussing the subject of the new birth with Nicodemus. It was during the course of the conversation, Jesus said to him, *"Verily, verily, I say unto thee, Except a man be born of water and of the Spirit, he cannot enter into the kingdom of God. That which is born of the flesh is flesh; and that which is born of the Spirit is spirit. Marvel not that I said unto thee, Ye must be born again,"* (John 3:5-7). Just prior to that Jesus said that a man must be *born again.*

I have talked to many people who believe being a Christian means *believing the story of Jesus* or *asking Jesus into your heart*, or *saying the sinner's prayer.* Unfortunately, for them, it means none of those things. If it does, why are these options not clearly spelled out in Scripture? Becoming a Christian means *being born from above*, by a supernatural act of God in which the Holy Spirit takes up residence within us, indwelling us for the remainder of our time here on earth.

Paul explains this for us in detail in Romans 6-8. Authentic believers walk after the Spirit, not after the flesh. He also states, *"For whosoever shall call upon the name of the Lord shall be saved,"* (Romans 10:13). Those who call upon the Name of the Lord and who are saved because of it should see a difference in their life. They should also note a greater desire to serve God. Paul states that those who are authentic believers should live different lives than those around them who are not believers. He also deftly tells us *how* to live that new life within. "*I beseech you therefore, brethren, by the mercies of God, that ye present your bodies a living sacrifice, holy, acceptable unto God, which is your reasonable service. And be not conformed to this world: but be ye transformed by the renewing of your mind, that ye may prove what is that good, and acceptable, and perfect, will of God,*" (Romans 12:1-2).

If you are not living your life in the above-prescribed way and you say that you are a Christian, it is time for some self-reflection. Look at yourself and see whether you submit yourself to Christ's Lordship. He is Lord regardless, but are you *willingly* submitting to that Lord-ship? If not, it is time for you to begin doing just that.

If you are *not* a believer, there is no magic statement that will make you one. You cannot simply pray a prayer of "come into my heart Lord Jesus" and you will have salvation. What needs to be done is for you to realize your utter helplessness before God. You need to real-ize that because of the fact that you are a sinner in that you have bro-ken God's Law, and that you have a sin nature, which helps you sin even when you do not want to do so, you are cut off from God. It is our sin, which has placed us on the road to hell. The only thing that will get us off that road is by *trusting* in the efficacious atonement of another.

Jesus Christ died an agonizingly painful, bloody death and by doing so took on God's wrath, the wrath that was meant for you and for me. Because He willingly allowed Himself to be killed and to be the reci-pient of God's wrath, God's righteous anger was spent during the time Jesus hung on Calvary's cross. In essence, He *became* sin for us, yet He had never sinned personally (cf. 2 Corinthians 5:21). Because **He** was literally *seen* as sin instead of us, we have the opportunity to become *righteous*. We do so by believing that Jesus died for us, yet did not have to, but because He died, we do not have to continue to die spiritually.

If we come to the point of realizing that we are completely helpless in our position before God, and if we come to know that Jesus died for us, when it should have been us, then we will begin to see the truth. The truth is *"...when we were yet without strength, in due time Christ died for the ungodly. For scarcely for a righteous man will one die: yet peradventure for a good man some would even dare to die. But God commendeth his love toward us, in that, while we were yet sinners, Christ died for us. Much more then, being now justified by his blood, we shall be saved from wrath through him,"* (Romans 5:6-9).

In understanding this truth, our eyes become open, just as did the thief's, who hung next to Jesus. With our eyes open, we become conscious of the fact that without Christ, we will continue on our current path toward hell. It is only when we see that we are helpless, and while we were still helpless, Jesus died for us. Once we see this, we realize that it is only in trusting in Jesus' death and resurrection that we gain salvation. It is a matter of *faith*, not of saying a "sinner's prayer," or walking down the aisle at church. It is literally *believing* or *trusting* the fact that Christ's death was **substitutionary** for *ours*. We should be facing God's wrath for all eternity in hell and we will, if we do not see that Jesus died in our place, in order that we might have eternal life.

Salvation is a *spiritual rebirth*. It is a transaction, which takes place in the spiritual realm. It happens when and only when, we *trust* in the atonement of Jesus' death. We place our trust in Him and His death, in essence, believing that His death was enough and salvation becomes ours.

Once salvation becomes ours, the Holy Spirit dwells within us and seals unto the day of redemption, (cf. Ephesians 1:14; 4:13-14; Romans 8; 1 Corinthians 6:19-20). We cannot lose our salvation once granted. The human responsibility is our obligation to *live* a life that pleases God. This can only be done by our constant submission to Him and His purposes.

Ultimately, having salvation is being *in relationship with Jesus Christ.* If you do not know Him, if you are not in relationship with Him, then you are not saved, no matter how many times you may have prayed the "sinner's prayer." What saves you is trusting in the finished work of Jesus Christ on your behalf. You must call out to Him, telling Him that you want to be able to trust His work on your behalf. I pray that before you have finished reading this book, you will do so if you have not done so already.

- Fred DeRuvo, May 2010

Introduction: the Church

It is important to understand from the outset that there are two terms primarily used to designate *church*. It is also vital to recognize which is which. In his book *Footsteps of the Messiah*, Dr. Arnold Fruchtenbaum states that the *visible* Church and the *invisible* Church are different in that the "*latter is the Body of the Messiah, composed of all true believers since Pentecost. It is sometimes referred to as the Universal Church. But the visible church is the local body or*

local church, which may have both believers and unbelievers. It includes all professing believers whether they really are or not. While the invisible Church has only believers, the visible church can have both."[1]
It is imperative as the reader moves through *this* book to appreciate this difference and keep it in mind. Most of the time, the discussion will center on the *invisible Church*. However, at times the *visible church* will be highlighted. Normally, the differences will be obvious because the references to the *visible church* will include mention of the *local body of believers.*

Individual vs. Universal

In the book of Revelation, chapters two through three, we read seven letters to seven specific churches:

1. *Ephesus*
2. *Smyrna*
3. *Pergamum*
4. *Thyatira*
5. *Sardis*
6. *Philadelphia*
7. *Laodicea*

The above churches are individual churches in Asia Minor, and therefore are part of the *visible church* and the authentic believers in each of those local bodies were part of the *invisible church*. This is fairly easy to determine from Scripture due to context of the individual passage. The *interpretation* of the passage however, is not quite so easy. Some biblical scholars believe that each church was chosen by the Holy Spirit that represent a specific epoch of history, with out current time period represented by the Laodicean church. Others believe that they were picked by the Holy Spirit because John, who penned the book of Revelation, had some type of direct connection with each church. This debate does not enter into this

---

[1] Arnold G. Fruchtenbaum *Footsteps of the Messiah* (Tustin: Ariel Ministries, 2004), 47

discussion. What matters is that the *visible church* should always be distinguished from the *invisible Church*.

Matthew 16:18 is where Christ references the fact that He will build His Church. Here He is speaking of the *invisible Church*, not the local bodies that *contain* both believers and professing believers (*the visible church*). In his first letter to the Corinthians, 1 Corinthians 12:13 when Paul speaks of the fact that believers are "*baptized into one body...*", he is referencing the *invisible Church* (the Body of Christ).

Matthew 18:17 speaks of the individual, or *visible church*. Here, Jesus is pointing out the rules to deal with problems in the local church. In other places in the New Testament like Acts 5:11 and 8:1, specific churches were mentioned. Whenever Paul or Peter are presenting doctrinal truth related to the *invisible* Church, it is the entire Body of authentic believers in view, yet at times, Paul speaks of specific congregations, such as the Corinthians in which he explains the rules for properly observing the Lord's Supper and more.

This book deals largely with the *invisible Church*. All true believers make up the *invisible Church*, and all true believers having been baptized into Christ's Body are partakers of the divine blessings, which stem from our spiritual union with Him. These blessings are there only for authentic Christians, not professing Christians. In that sense, these blessings do not extend to the *visible church* per se, but only to those authentic believers within the *visible church*.

Lewis Sperry Chafer notes 33 divine blessings, or riches of His grace, that belong to true believers. We will spend some time going over these blessings later on in this book. Again, these blessings are reserved *only* for those who are authentic believers, those who have been baptized in Christ's Body.

Satan works to accomplish essentially two things directed to the Christian:

1. He endeavors to cause the authentic believer to sin and doubt God as often as possible, and
2. He works to keep the authentic believer blind to the multitude of blessings found *in Christ*

Masters at Knowing What Ails Us

Normally, Christians are very well aquainted with the *former*. We all know too well what it means to sin, and the temptations that usually *precede* our sin. What we are not as well aquainted with are the areas in which we are blessed. We know that we have salvation. We know that we are baptized into Christ's Body. We know that He is our Advocate against Satan who accuses us constantly. We know that we will one day be free of our sin nature, and because of that, we know that we will be forever free from *sin*. We know that we will be *perfected*, found to be completely conformed to His image upon our deaths. We further know that by His strength, we have the power to *avoid* sin. We also know that the Holy Spirit indwells us, and has sealed us unto the day of redemption.

The preceding list of things are wonderful, and in fact, in and of themselves are things with which we could spend hours contemplating and praising God over. These are *not* all the blessings that we have in Christ Jesus, and in fact, these represent but a small portion, though a *tremendously important* portion. Is there more? If there is, are we to know it? If we are to know it, what then? If there are more blessings of divine riches available to us, why *don't* we know about them?

I believe it is solely because Satan does not want us to know. This certainly does not mean that he is more powerful than God, able to keep the truth of God's Word from us. The problem is that too many Christians today do not study for themselves God's Word, and too many preachers and teachers do not spend enough time equipping the saints on the divine riches He has provided for us now.

Satan of course wants *no one* to be saved. He hates the fact that salvation is available to anyone, but his hatred knows no bounds when a person whose eyes are open to the gospel, comes to embrace the truth of that gospel. That person, now an authentic believer, is indwelt by the Holy Spirit and sealed unto the day of redemption. There is nothing Satan can do to make that person *unsaved*. It cannot happen, in spite of the belief put forth by some that salvation *can* be lost. The most Satan can do is make their lives miserable and he does this in a number of ways as mentioned; by causing the believer to sin, and by keeping valuable truth from him.

This book is written to help bring that truth to you. It is in God's Word, which is where the information for this book was taken. As often is the case though, without explanation, God's Word can unfortunately be *words* that we merely read and hear, but fail to comprehend. The reason we do not understand them is often due to our own failure to seek the Lord during our study.

The truth of God's Word is there and available. Its riches are infinite, which is exactly why Satan wants to keep us from it. He knows all too well that God's truth from God's Word means the difference between defeat and victory for the believer. Is it any wonder that Satan prefers that we know little to nothing of God's Word? Yet there it is; the *only* absolute truth that exists.

As you move through this book, please do what the Bereans did regarding Paul's message. In the seventeenth chapter of Acts, they heard Paul, and then went right back to Scripture. There they studied to determine if what Paul had taught was *accurate*. Do not take my word for what is presented in these pages. You have an obligation to determine the veracity of these words, based purely on the testimony of Scripture. This is what Paul refers to when he says to Timothy that he needs to rightly divide God's Word (cf. 2 Timothy 2:15). Barring that, you will simply be reading another book (this one), which may or may not have truth. Only God's Word will tell you by either confirming or negating what is taught herein.

Chapter 1
Child Abuse?

C onsider this scene. You are walking by a community park, and you hear wailing. The wailing is coming from a child, around the age of ten to twelve years of age. You have no idea what happened, but here is what you see and hear: the child is in emotional agony, berating himself because of something he apparently did to another child at the park, during play. In a moment of exuberance, and without thinking, he pushed another child down during a game of touch football. The child that was pushed to the ground twisted her ankle and was in a good deal of pain. You move closer and you are able to see that the hurt girl has a swollen ankle, and surprisingly enough, while there are tears coming down her cheeks, her crying amounts to sniffling and quiet sobs due to the pain. Her mother and father comfort her as they gingerly wrap her ankle.

Self-Denigration

You turn your attention to the boy who is crying loudly. What alarms you though is not the fact that he is crying, but what you hear him say *as* he cries. He is obviously remonstrating himself for the fact that he pushed the girl down and caused her pain. *"I can't believe how stupid I am!"* you hear him moan. *"I didn't mean it, but I can't help it because of how rotten I am inside! I don't deserve to be here or enjoy anything in life, because of how bad I am!! I'm really, REALLY sorry for what I did! There is no excuse for it and I deserve to be punished severely!"*

You glance over at the parents and they are both looking at their son, obviously approving of his feelings of worthlessness. Their expressions tell their son that he is doing the right thing, and in fact, the more he continues to exhibit this type of behavior, the more approval he receives from his parents. Eventually, you turn away, and continue in the direction you were heading before the scene in the park sidetracked you.

Though the above situation is not real, it serves to make a point. Most of us would become slightly annoyed to angry if we actually came across a scene like that, wouldn't we? We might begin to believe that there was something akin to child abuse happening behind closed doors. Let's face it, if the parents obviously approved of their son reacting as he did, and even encouraging him to come down on himself harder, then the natural question is *what does go on behind closed doors where no one else can see*?

I remember years ago working in a shoe store at a mall. Most of the people who came into shop were enjoyable and the staff was great as well.

Emotional Abuse

However, one day, a woman came in with two young children. She was slightly unkempt and seemed to be perpetually exasperated. The other thing I noticed about her was when I spoke with her or her with me; she never once looked me in the eye. Something just felt wrong.

She kept the two young kids on an emotional as well as physical "leash," holding their hands – one on each side of her – the entire time they were there. I glanced at the boy who in spite of the fact that he was neatly dressed with hair that was combed, he had a slight black eye. This could have been due to anything since I knew that young boys like to play and play hard.

Neither the young girl nor boy said one word the entire time they were in the store. The mother spoke for them, sighed a lot, and in general, just seemed annoyed *at* them, even though they did nothing to warrant her annoyed response.

I was in my very early twenties at the time, and the only thing I could figure out was that the woman was annoying me. Her very presence was irritating. She said she wanted to try on a pair of shoes and so I headed back to the storeroom to pick up the pair she wanted. As I walked away, she began talking with the children. I glanced back, and saw that they were at attention, focusing on every word she said. I could not hear what she said, but her tone more than suggested that she was not happy with them. I could not figure out why, since they had been perfect angels ever since they walked into the store.

I brought out the shoes, the woman tried them on and decided she didn't like them and with the two children, left the store. It was odd.

My heart went out to those two kids and I really did not know why.

A short while later, I went on my break and headed out into the mall. I noticed the same woman with these two kids not far from the store, and there she sat, with the two kids in front of her. They were intently looking at her and I saw her mouth moving, but was too far away to hear anything. It was obvious that this was not a happy discussion and for the life of me, I could not figure out what was going on. It must have been something they may have done earlier.

Child Abuser?

It was not until later that evening that I realized what might have been taken place was a form of child abuse. Everything this woman did was done to make these two young kids feel *bad about them-selves*. They could do nothing right; everything was wrong, and she would not let them off the hook about any of it.

I also realized why I had become annoyed with the woman. She had gotten under my skin because of the fact that I sensed something was wrong. Now that I have taught in the public school system, I have come to the realization that she might have been a child abuser. Of course, just because a parent is annoyed with her kids does not mean that child abuse is taking place, however, with what I know *now* at this stage in my life, it is very likely that this was the case.

I was flying somewhere a few years ago and directly across the row from me was a youngish mother with two small boys. One of the boys was probably around 5 or 6 and the other was still in a car seat. As soon as the mother took the seats with her boys, she turned to the older boy and immediately started giving him instructions. Bearing in mind that the flight was taking off in the very early evening, the mother however, was intent to have the older boy "go to sleep." She would say, "*Now you be quiet. Stop wiggling around. Put your head down and go to sleep.*" The boy would oblige her for a very short while and then would get itchy, unable to sit still. The mother would come down on him again and the cycle would repeat itself.

Eventually, the boy – completely unable to sleep (wonder why!) – would be unable to stay still in his seat. He obviously had energy, yet the mother was only interested in dealing with the younger boy, who was in the car seat.

It Was Getting on My Nerves

The constant commands to the older boy were starting to get on my nerves. I turned to my wife and stated as much. I was in the aisle seat and the older boy was in an aisle seat across from me. After hearing the mother berate the son for what seemed like an eternity, I finally blurted out, "*Is it all right if I talk to him?*" The mother nodded her head, and so I thankfully began talking to the little boy. He had a lot to tell me and I was so glad that he could get it out.

He was excited about going to see his daddy (I believe he was in the military). When he talked about his daddy, his smile became very big. He told me what he did in school, and he even told me he was a Jehovah's Witness. Occasionally, the mother would interrupt with "*Don't be loud,*" or something else and I would gently and good-naturedly assure her that he was fine. I'm sorry to say that I actually wanted to say to her in no uncertain terms, "SHUT UP!" but I kept my peace and did not end up sinning at least outwardly, though within I had screamed at her a number of times.

Finally, the plane landed and we got off. As I got up to disembark, the boy looked up, told me his name, and said, "*Don't forget me!*" with a beautiful smile on his face. I told him I wouldn't, but didn't really know what he meant by that. It does not matter because I pray for him every time I think of him.

In the aforementioned situations, I cannot think of any normal person who would *approve* of any of the three situations. If you saw a young boy in a community park who spent that much time and energy berating himself, with parents who stood by silently encouraging him to do *more*, you would be tempted to step in and do something.

At the same time, if you witnessed a person who seemed as though she ruled her kids with a rod of iron (think, "Mommy Dearest"), you would become angered and want to do something to change the situation.

In the last situation, you might do what I did, just to ease the situation for that young boy, whose mother was too preoccupied with her *sleeping* son to pay any attention to the one who was awake. That situation left alone would have become interminable for that older boy, and because of it, who knows how his mother might have disciplined him later for not obeying her very unreasonable demands on the airplane trip.

Righteous Indignation

One thing is common to all three of these situations. In each case, you would become righteously indignant. How dare any parent treat their child like that! If the parent really loved the child, how could they let him berate himself, emotionally abuse them into submission, or make unrealistic demands on him? It is not fair and it is something that a normal parent who truly loved their child, would never do. Of this, you are sure.

Loving parents do their best to raise their children with *love*. It means plenty of encouragement, nurturing, and wisdom is used in the process of childrearing. Good parents do not emotionally browbeat or physically mistreat their children. At the same time, these same parents will chastise their children when necessary, because they know that if they do not, they are not doing the child any favors. Healthy discipline is part of the process of raising children so that they become healthy adults.

Even when our children do something that does not make us proud and may even wind up embarrassing themselves, we may get upset, but we do not disown them. Ultimately, we want our children to know they are *loved*, and we want them to know that they are *accountable*.

Yet, why is it, when it comes to God, our Father, there are many Christians who believe God is just like that? However, there is no indication from Scripture that God revels in emotional abuse He sees in His children, nor does He delight in putting unreasonable expectations on us. We believe that if we do not *show* Him how bad we feel about our sin, how repugnant it makes us feel, how terrible we are because of it, then He will not be pleased with us. If we are not taking the time to beat ourselves up, then God not only does *not* approve, but also will send some calamity on us to get our attention. How is it possible that we can actually believe these attributes accurately represent God's reaction *toward* His very own children?

This is what some people within Christendom are making the Christian walk. They do this by continually focusing on their sin, their failures, and their lack of consistency. Why? I believe it has everything to do with Satan's way of using the sin nature to make us believe that we must either *earn* salvation, or *earn* God's continued favor.

Satan Loves to Keep us in the Dark
Think of it. Almost all cults are based on a form of salvation that centers on the belief that salvation comes to us via *works*. While some folks might admit and agree that salvation is also by *faith*, works are part of the deal and I am not talking about works as an *evidence* of salvation. They mean that works is *part of the actual equation of salvation*.

If Satan cannot keep us from receiving salvation, he will work to distort its meaning to us. He endeavors to keep us from appreciating our standing in Christ, because once we start to understand our true position in Christ, along with the fact that Christ has freed us from the law of sin and death, we can then truly begin to grow in Christ, maturing spiritually. Prior to this, we are normally doing two things:

1. *Living licentiously, not really caring about how much or how often we sin, because we believe that Christ took care of our sin at Calvary, or*
2. *We are too focused on our sin, so that it becomes our all-consuming focus.*

In either of the above scenarios, we fall short of God's perfect will. We wind up ignoring our true position in Christ altogether, instead focusing on ourselves. Most would agree without hesitation that Christians living in licentiousness is wrong. There is no doubt about that to anyone who knows anything about Scripture, especially Paul's teaching to the Corinthians.

However, these same individuals will overemphasize the sin in our life, because this somehow *feels* as though it is commendable. Many Christians believe that it is good to feel terrible about our sin; to believe that we must spend extended periods of time *mourning* for the fact that we put Jesus Christ on the cross, eventually coming to a point of spiritual brokenness.

The *worse* we feel about ourselves, the more *holy* we believe we are becoming. I believe that this stems from a number of errors, chief of which combines how God deals with the nation of Israel and the Church. People, who are unable to see these as two separate entities, consistently mix up the fact that how God dealt with Israel is *not* how He deals with the Church.

Let's be clear here though, because I do not want to be misconstrued. There is only *one* way of salvation. In fact, there has only ever been one method of salvation, and it has always been through faith in God.

This is the only way that He has ever been able to count anyone righteous at all, through *faith*.

Abraham believed God and it was counted to him as righteousness (cf. Genesis 15). What was counted to him as righteousness? It was his *faith* or his *trust* in God's Word. When God saw Abraham's faith – the fact that Abraham purely and simply took God at His Word – God blessed him by declaring him righteous. Nowhere in Scripture do I see a place where God ever rescinded that declaration.

It has always been by faith, starting with Adam and Eve, through Enoch, Noah, Abraham, Lot, Paul, Peter, and everyone through today. It will be by faith until the Lord Jesus Christ returns in glory, taking charge of this, His planet. Adam and Eve sinned because they failed to continue to *believe* God's Word. Their sin began in their hearts and the actual eating of the forbidden fruit was simply the outward action of the inward sin.

With that said, please know that there is no contradiction at all with God's desire, and purposes for Israel and those for God the Son's Body (the Church). His purposes for each of these two entities go beyond salvation. God has decreed that each has a unique purpose in the course of His will, neither conflicting with the other. Salvation is the *exact same thing* for each, but God's purposes beyond salvation are dissimilar.

This is no difference between how members of each group receive salvation. The difference is centered on each group's *purpose*. So while you and I are saved in the exact same manner, God's will and purposes for you *after* you receive salvation is far different than His will and purposes for me.

So how does *not* seeing Israel and the Church as two different entities create a potential problem? We will see that very thing in our next chapter.

Chapter 2

Like Yourself Much?

F eeling terrible about yourself? Good. There is nothing better than believing that you *never* measure up, are *never* good enough, or that your sin is always before you, and that God is one-step away from disowning you...*all the time*. Such is the "wisdom" of some who believe they are called to preach to Christians about their constant failures. They seem to delight in bringing either themselves or their listeners to great displays of anguish and tears of sorrow. For it is this, they believe, that proves that repentance has occurred.

It has become disheartening to hear the constant verbal flagellations that the Church is *corrupt*, filled with *sin* and in need of some good ol' *purification*. Many believe that the coming persecution (or make that the *growing* persecution) is designed by God to bring about this purification of Christ's *Body*, His *Church*. Frankly, that is absurd, because it seems to be completely *unbiblical*.

Paul tells us in the book of Romans that we are:

- *justified*
- *righteous*
- *glorified*
- *being sanctified*

The Church is NOT Israel

The problem as I see it is that those who consistently mix *Israel* and the *Church* are often the ones who believe that just as God had to *purify* Israel in the Old Testament numerous times, He must do the same thing to the Church. The difficulty though is that God always dealt with Israel as a nation. In other words, when there was a problem in the camp of the Israelites, the entire nation suffered.

For instance, in Numbers 14, we are familiar with the situation in which many individuals in the camp of Israel complained against Moses because of the report of the 12 spies. Ten of them did not believe the Lord. Why? It was because these individuals were *rebels.* This attitude left them filled with doubt toward God and His ability to fight for them. As such, they were completely opposed to any work that God was doing in their midst, no matter how many times they witnessed His power through deliverance. They were not men after God's heart. They lived in *unbelief,* never having believed the Lord at all. While they enjoyed the bounty of God's provision repeatedly, they resolutely refused to acquiesce to His reign. They went along for the ride with an unbelieving heart. They wanted out of Egypt and went with an attitude of unbelief. It was because of this, that they were unable to believe that God would give them the victory if they entered the Promised Land. They had no confidence in God because they lived in unbelief.

What One Suffered They All Suffered

Two of the spies - Joshua and Caleb - believed that the Promised Land could be taken because God would provide the victory. This did not matter to the people because they became convinced (or at least did not argue) by those who complained. It was because of this that God denied the entire camp access to the Promised Land, even though not all people sided with the complainers. Nonetheless, the entire camp wandered for 40 years until every last man of that generation who had complained against God died in the wilderness. When Israel did finally enter the Land, Joshua and Caleb were there with them.

In Joshua 7:1-15, we read of the sin of one man, which caused the entire camp to suffer for it. Despite the command not to take any spoils of war, Achan takes a few items and hides them in his tent, unbeknownst to Joshua or anyone else in the camp. The camp wound up losing their battle against Ai because of this sin.

Please note the very first verse of Joshua 7, which states, "*But the children of Israel committed a trespass in the accursed thing: for Achan, the son of Carmi, the son of Zabdi, the son of Zerah, of the tribe of Judah, took of the accursed thing: and the anger of the LORD was kindled against the children of Israel.*"

Note that in this verse, God holds the entire nation of Israel guilty, even though it was one man - Achan - who committed the trespass. The full camp suffered the loss and was on the receiving end of God's anger. Eventually, after the loss, Joshua rent his clothes and sought the Lord. Joshua spent all day with his face before the Lord, beseeching the Lord for an answer. Eventually, God responds with this: "*Joshua, Get thee up; wherefore liest thou thus upon thy face?*" (v. 10b)

God continued saying, "Israel hath sinned, and they have also trans-
gressed my covenant which I commanded them: for they have even
taken of the accursed thing, and have also stolen, and dissembled also,
and they have put it even among their own stuff." (v. 11)

Do you see how God holds the entire camp of Israel responsible for
what one individual did? This is not the case with the Church for any
number of reasons and the idea that the Church needs to be purified
is an insidious form of false-piety. In other words, what is ultimately
being stated is that Christ's blood sacrifice was not good enough to
cleanse His Bride, therefore we as Christians, need to help Christ by
rending our clothes, sitting in ashes dressed in sackcloth, and we
must be willing to beat ourselves up emotionally, in spite of the fact
that Christ does not.

What I have found is that the majority of people who espouse this
seem to be individuals who have conformed to the Covenant or Re-
formed position. They believe that the invisible Church has replaced
Israel and that God is completely done in His dealings with Israel at
all. They are unable to see a difference between the nation of Israel
and the Church in Scripture. In spite of the fact that my sin - *past*,
present, and *future* - has not only already been *forgiven*, but is completely *gone*, too many people believe that those within the (*visible*)
Church are corrupt and therefore, have corrupted the (*invisible*)
Church (which is Christ's Bride). This is insane, because Christ cannot ever receive a Bride stained with sin! The only thing my sin can
do is hurt my relationship with God until such a time as I sincerely
confess it to Him!

Sin is <u>NEVER</u> Okay!
Let me be exceedingly clear here. I want there to be no misunders-
tanding. As a believer, I am to *never* have a laissez-faire attitude
about my own personal sin, for it was that sin that put Jesus Christ on
the cross. Because of that, I am to see my sin as *reprehensible* because of what it prompted God to do for me. However, it is one thing

to see my *sin* as reprehensible and quite another to see *myself* as re-prehensible!

I can *never* look at my sin as if it is no big deal, because it *is a big deal*. It is nothing short of *lawlessness*. It is allowing *self* to be glorified, in-stead of God, who deserves ALL the glory. Whenever I sin - either knowingly or unknowingly - God is *grieved*. Yet, He does *not* hate me!

When I sin, at that instant, the fellowship that I enjoy with Him is harmed, but not broken, until I *confess* my sin, *sincerely* from the heart. It is at *that* point, that fellowship is reestablished. This fellow-ship continues until I sin again. This is the unfortunate aspect of be-ing a Christian who continues to retain the *sin nature* (which is *ALL* believers). Though God has given me a completely *new spirit,* and a *new nature*, which has made me a *new creation*, my sin nature is *ever-present*. It has *not* died, or been removed, and it *never* takes a holi-day.

Because the sin nature is ever-present within all of us, it continues to try to force us to do what we do *not* want to do. It is because of this unfortunate situation that sin is *always at the door*, always seeking its way, instead of what *God* wants us to do.

Even in spite of the continued presence of the sin nature, authentic Christians are referred to as "saints" throughout the New Testament epistles from Paul, Peter and others. The first chapter of Ephesians explains that we were chosen to be *holy*. If this is read with the wrong understanding, it will be taken to mean that there is a *choice* made by us - to be holy or not to be holy. The reality is that as au-thentic Christians, we *already are holy*. Why? Because the new spirit that God has placed within me *is holy* and *completely sinless*. That new spirit within me can *never sin*. However, I *can* choose to follow the dictates of my sin nature, thereby *committing sin*.

When I *do* sin, the new creation within me is *still* in Christ, *not* participating in that sin with my *flesh*. What I have done though is moved from being *in Christ* with my mind, and instead, I have followed my *flesh* to commit sin. Though I commit sin, the new creation that God has *made* me does *not sin*. This is exactly why Paul can say in all truthfulness that "*Even when we were dead in sins, hath quickened us together with Christ, (by grace ye are saved;) And hath raised us up together, and made us sit together in heavenly places in Christ Jesus,*" (Ephesians 2:5-6). We are now seated with Christ in the heavenly realms. It is because our sinless nature as part of our new creation is *in Christ*. That new nature never leaves Christ to participate in the sin of our flesh. These two natures never meet. Even after we die, our sin nature is eradicated, so it still never meets our new nature.

The New Creation Does Not Sin

This is exactly why John says that those who are *in Christ* are done with sin. "*Whosoever abideth in him sinneth not: whosoever sinneth hath not seen him, neither known him,*" (1 John 3:6). What John is saying here is that those who *abide* in Christ, do *not* sin. This means that the new spirit God has given us *abides in Christ*. That is our *position*.

We can benefit from that *union* with Christ, or we can choose to walk after the flesh. When we walk after the flesh, we *sin*, however our new creation does *not*. As we endeavor in His strength to walk as Christ walked, we will not fulfill the lusts of the flesh, but will instead benefit from our new spirit, which is joined to (or *abides in*) Christ.

Paul teaches this to us in the book of Romans as well. When we become Christians, we are baptized into HIS Body. How is it possible for His Body to become contaminated by sin? It is impossible. The new spirit that God placed within me is already seated with Christ in the heavenlies. It is incapable of sinning, yet as I have *clearly* stated, in my flesh, I can and do follow the dictates of my sin nature from time to time. However, my sinful flesh is *not* part of Christ's Body. It is the flesh, which means it IS corrupt, dying, and *will* die. The new spirit that God gave me will *never* die.

Based on this, how is it possible that the Church can ever be considered *impure*? To believe that is to believe that Christ's sacrifice was not good enough, that His Blood could not cleanse completely, and that as believers who are still able to sin, we are capable of making Christ's Body *impure*. This is so far off base that it is difficult to avoid reacting in annoyance or anger to this error.

The people who *clamor* for, *yell* for, and *demand* that believers need to spend more time on our knees in repentance, pleading with God to forgive us (something He has *already* done), do not - in my opinion - understand the doctrine of eternal security, or unmerited grace, or salvation through *faith* alone, by *grace* alone, in *Christ* alone, or the fact that we have been richly blessed by our union with Christ, though they *SAY* they do. I also believe that these same individuals are constantly confusing *tares* with *wheat*. They see the *tares* in the *visible* Church (not that we can know who they are), and they believe that because of them, the *invisible* Church needs to purify itself. This is simply not true, because the *tares* are *not* part of the *invisible* Church (which is Christ's true BRIDE) at all!

Keeping the Sin List Short
Believers are *required* to keep a very short list of sins. As the Holy Spirit brings our individual sin to our attention, we are to immediately agree and confess our sin, not with our lips, but from the heart. We should never want to sin, or ever believe that "small" sins are okay with God. We should never wink at sin, nor take our standing before Christ for granted. Sin is sin and it is *never* under any circumstances acceptable to God! I cannot make that any clearer.

However, we as Christians, unlike what some evangelists teach, do not need to wallow in self-condemning feelings for ourselves over our sin. The natural tendency of fallen human beings is to either think that sin is not a big deal, or we fall into the trap of believing that unless we feel terrible, and unless we beat ourselves up emotionally (or even physically!), we have not truly repented. This borders on heresy in my opinion, because it attempts to *add* to the existing purifying reality of salvation. This attitude feeds our pride, which in turn feeds and gives rise to sin.

All *authentic* believers understand that salvation cannot be earned. Yet too many have fallen into the mistake of believing that we must *work* to *maintain* our salvation, as if God is incapable of doing that Himself. Folks, the fact is that *if* we have to help God maintain our salvation, then we do not actually have salvation at all.

Yes, I am *obligated* to confess my sin. I am also obligated to keep my eyes on Jesus. Focusing on my sin takes my eyes off Jesus and puts them squarely on *me*, where they do not belong.

We read in 1 John 3:3-4, "*Beloved, now are we the sons of God, and it doth not yet appear what we shall be: but we know that, when he shall appear, we shall be like him; for we shall see him as he is. And every man that hath this hope in him purifieth himself, even as he is pure.*"

So what is it that actually *purifies* the believer? Beyond this, what exactly does it mean to *purify* ourselves? Does it not seem clear that when we have our thoughts on Jesus, we cannot be thinking of fulfilling the sin nature's demands? The two are *incompatible*. We cannot be focusing on Jesus while at the same time, focusing on ways to fulfill the desires of the flesh. It is *impossible*. It is the focusing on Jesus that purifies the believer's thoughts, words, and deeds.

Self-Aggrandizement

Focusing on how *terrible* I am, how *worthless* I am, how much of a *worm* I am, is nothing but *self-aggrandizement*, in the guise of external religious piety. While it certainly has a *form of religion*, it does not produce the change that only Christ can produce. Beating ourselves up does not produce godliness. In fact, what it does is create a *false sense of spiritual maturity*, which is actually spiritual *poverty* born of pride (cf. Colossians 2:23), and normally comes out as *arrogance*. While we may believe that we are growing in our faith, because of emotional pain or trauma for our sin, all we are doing is spending time *endorsing* the evil inherent in the sin nature and the flesh.

If we truly believed that Christ's redemption was *perfectly sufficient*, and that He is the Author and Perfector of our faith, we would not be trying so hard to drum up feelings of worthlessness within ourselves. Instead, we would be determined to focus on Him, and His life within us. Doing this does more to bring about spiritual maturity than wallowing in the false sense of worthlessness that comes by focusing on *self*.

God has freed me from the Law of sin and death (cf. Romans 6-8). He lives within me and because of that, I *can* overcome sin if I rely on Him and His strength. Because I will never do it perfectly in this life, does not negate the fact that I *am* a Christian, nor does it somehow sully Christ or His Bride. That is absurd, and the quicker believers get to the point of realizing that beating ourselves up is wrong, because it denies the full efficacy of Christ's redemption, the quicker we begin focusing on the reality of our new birth and His presence within us. It is nothing but a form of godliness without the power.

As a final point for now, remember this from 1 John 3: "*but we know that, when he shall appear, we shall be like him*"? What does *that* statement *mean*? Doesn't it mean that when I die, I will *instantly* become as He is? If so, then that means that in the instant my soul leaves my body and stands before Him, I will be like Him. Funny, but John does not say that we have to repent and become filled with self-denigration. He says we will BE like Him. In other words, it will happen *apart* from us. It will happen because *HE MAKES IT HAPPEN*.

Christians need to listen to and understand that truth. There is a huge difference between TARES and WHEAT. The TARES will NEVER be believers (WHEAT), and the WHEAT will NEVER be TARES (unbelieving frauds).

We *cannot* see the *invisible* Church. We can only see the *VISIBLE* Church, which includes all the professing Christians, along with the TARES. It is the INVISIBLE Church that consists only of WHEAT, no TARES, no professing Christian, just WHEAT who are authentic Christians.

Persecution Separates

While some Christians firmly believe that persecution is what cleanses and purifies the Church, I disagree vehemently. It is NOT persecution, which purifies the Church because the Church is already pure. What persecution DOES is separate the sheep from the goats. The TARES cannot handle persecution, while the WHEAT cannot nor will not run from it.

Chapter 3

Blinded

So far, we have discussed several aspects of what it means to be a Christian; an *authentic* Christian, not someone who simply *claims* to be a Christian. With the exception of most Emergent Churches today (you know, the Seeker-friendly churches that de-emphasize truth, provide food and offer "rock" concerts every Sunday morning...all for His glory of course), it is relatively easy to find churches that preach about sin.

Many pastors have no difficulty with the subject of our sin nature because it is one thing that people share in *common*, whether they will admit or not. The sin nature is at the heart of our sinful behavior and even as Christians, we continue to *possess* this same sin nature, which is reason enough to believe that we will never be sinless in this life. The sin nature continues to attempt to wreak havoc in our lives by causing temptation to become overbearing, or even making temptation out of ordinary situations.

Bad to the Bone

It is extremely easy to discuss how bad people are, and how woefully short we fall. This does not simply apply to the *unsaved* either. It is often liberally applied to the *believer*. Many sermons from authentic (conservative) Christian pastors have to do with *holiness*. We are told to be *holy*, as Christ is *holy*. However, we too often tend to think of holiness in terms of *experience* as opposed to a *state of being*.

The New Testament alone is filled with warnings against continuing in sin and we are taught that we must heed the warning of the Holy Spirit within us in order that God would be glorified in and through us. These are good and necessary subjects to discuss; nevertheless, it appears as though the other side of the coin is too often left out of the equation and it is my contention that if this other side were included in more sermons, there would be a greater understanding of our true position in Christ, which I believe would naturally result in *less sin*.

Sinners to the End

We all know what sin is and we all know that we *are* sinners. Those folks who believe that they have actually achieved a state of sinless perfection are only kidding themselves. They are woefully unaware of what the Scriptures teach regarding the sin nature and the sin that it *can* and *does* help to create. Sin is still a problem for authentic believers and always will be in this life. It will not be until I die that my sin nature be sloughed off.

Anyone can get up and preach about the subject of sin and how reprehensible it is, and many do just that very thing. We think of

Charles Finney and how he was known for literally scaring people out of hell and into heaven. On the other hand, how often do you hear a message telling you all about the *blessings* that you enjoy in Christ, as believers? While some may allude to this subject, it is not often dealt with *systematically*, *seriously*, or in *detail*. Why is this the case? I believe there are a number of reasons that this subject is not broached that often.

1. *It is extremely difficult to appreciate all the benefits of our union with Christ, which we do not experience fully here and now.*
2. *It is far easier to teach about the negative aspects of the Christian's daily walk, than the positives.*
3. *It may send the wrong message causing people to think that they do not have to pay attention to their sin.*
4. *It is easier to get people to do things if they are constantly made to feel that their walk with Christ is just not good enough. In other words, guilt works better than praise.*

These problems and others like them keep authentic believers from understanding the reality of our present walk with Christ from *God's perspective*. Not knowing about these things – the *blessings* of being united with Christ – keep us in the dark about some very important aspects of what it means to *have* salvation.

Satan Never Sleeps
The greater reality here is that because this knowledge is not routinely disseminated in sermons, books, and teachings; there must be something that works very hard to keep this information from us. I believe that "something" is none other than Satan himself, along with the countless minions who serve him as their lord and master.

We know that Satan obviously blinds unsaved people (cf. 2 Corinthians 4:4), but what we do not often consider is how *badly* he is able to blind *authentic* believers! Satan has a tremendous amount to gain by keeping authentic believers in the dark. If he can get us to focus primarily on our *sin*, our *corruption*, and our lack of spiritual maturity, then he has already won many battles. While we know he will *not* win the war (and has already effectively *lost* because of Calvary), the nature of his insidious attacks through *blindness* should cause alarm in each and every believer.

This is not normally the case though. Most Christians try, try, try, but eventually get to a point of throwing up their hands and just kind of living their Christian life as best they can, or they spend their Christian lives in a debilitating state of always feeling less than, or never fully accepted, often recommitting their lives to Christ numerous times. This is directly because we do not know the *whole* story connected to our salvation. We only know part of it, the part that focuses in on our *sin* and what comes *after this life*. We are unaware of the blessings we have in Christ from which we benefit *now* and we are certainly unaware of the fact that there are over thirty (yes, *thirty*), *divine riches* that God in Christ *has already bestowed on us*. These are available *now* for our growth and for His glory.

This reality is tragic and there is no excuse for it, except the excuse of *ignorance*. When we think of Satan, we generally think in terms of his outright *attacks* on the believer. We think of the man Job from the book by the same name, and all that Satan was *allowed* to do to him. We consider Paul and the events that transpired in his life *after* he became a Christian. We reflect on all that he went through, and we wonder how he was able to stand up under it. Of course, it was due *only* to God's strength.

We think of the early Christians who died for Christ, often painfully, with no remorse evidenced by their executioners, and we wonder what it was about them that allowed them to stand in surety of knowing that Christ was with them? It is the fact that these individuals understood far more than the average Christian does currently, about the *Last Days* of human history before our Lord returns in power and victory. While we as Christians are very familiar with our sin, we plainly do not understand how spiritually *healthy* we are in Christ. It is a subject about which we are largely ignorant, and that is the way Satan likes it. This needs to change and it can only change through the careful and prayerful studying of God's Word.

Satan Wants Less – God Wants More
While Satan wants us blind to the benefits of being *in Christ*, the Holy Spirit has other plans and to that end, has provided many blessings that are ours in Christ *now*. While most authentic believers spend an inordinate amount of time focusing on their failures and downfalls, the Holy Spirit yearns to point out the multitude of *blessings* we have in Christ. It is *not* focusing on our sin that makes us holy. It is in understanding our true position in Christ, which promotes the sense of our holiness. In fact, I am convinced that if we allow the Holy Spirit to teach us not only what our position *is* in Christ, but all the benefits that are ours in Him, we would sin far less than we do now. This would be a natural outcome.

Let's be clear here. I am *not* talking about any "name it, claim it," philosophy or "how to get rich" scheme. This has nothing to do with that false doctrine. The benefits that we have and should enjoy fully are in the *spiritual realm*, not in the *physical*. I cannot *claim* anything from God, except that which He has already given me.

I cannot *tell* Him to do anything thinking that if I simply have enough faith, it will be done. This is not Christianity. It is viewing God as if He were my personal Genie. He is *not* in any way, shape, or form, my butler, genie, or slave. God forbid!

I am enslaved *to Him*, because of my union with Jesus. Because I am enslaved to Him, the only thing I should ever be concerned about is fulfilling *His* will for my life. I am here because He has things for me to do, and my focus had better be on *those* things, not what I want out of life!

God's will is clearly delineated in God's Word. His will is twofold:

- *To do the good works He has foreordained for me*
- *To avoid sinning in order to recognize His great mercy, love, and grace*

If we stop to consider the fact that if we love God with all our heart and love our neighbor as ourselves, we will be doing those two bulleted items above. God recreates God the Son's character within us by our fulfillment of the two things listed above. It would be ludicrous to believe that He wanted me to do those things in my own strength.

Since I am unable to keep the Law in my own strength, how could He possibly expect me to do things that glorify Him after I am saved, *in my own strength*? If it were possible, it would lead to pride. This is obviously not true since He has provided so many divine riches in the spiritual realm for authentic Christians, His children. If I was expected to complete His will in my own strength, the divine riches are not necessary.

Blessings in the Now

The blessings that are mine in the spiritual realm are mine *for this earthly walk.* They are not there merely for eternity. In other words, the blessings that are mine in Christ Jesus are mine *now.* Their purpose is to help me *overcome* sin and fulfill other aspects of His will in the way, which glorifies Him.

The tragedy is that Satan desperately wants us to remain in the dark with respect to these blessings. He knows that once the authentic believer starts to understand His true position in Christ, and begins to realize the many wonderful blessings we have in Him, we will move further and further away from the kingdom of darkness because we will be living more and more for Christ. Is this what you want, or do you want to remain blinded to the blessings, believing that you are not worthy, and that you should be satisfied in remaining ignorant? If you think this, then may I respectfully suggest that you get on your knees, with an open Bible and pray for God's enlightenment regarding the divine riches that we share by being united with Christ?

Chapter 4

Spiritual Mediocrity

Too many authentic Christians are completely unaware of the true standing we enjoy in Jesus Christ. Because of this, we fail on many fronts and those failures become our *focus*. Satan enjoys and prefers that this should be our daily experience. Under no circumstances does he *ever* want us to become aware of our true standing in Christ. If we did, we would be able to live *above* the spiritual mediocrity that we have cultivated for ourselves over the years. Does it make sense to you that one of Satan's biggest ploys is to keep the authentic Christian blinded to the truth of our standing in Christ?

Satan's Greatest Tool

Satan has a great deal to lose and the Christian has a great deal to gain once our eyes open to that truth. While it is easy to think of attacks of the enemy in terms of external *trials, persecutions, tribulations,* people coming against us as *liars, haters,* those who tell *rumors* about us, and more, we rarely if ever consider the fact that one of the greatest tools Satan ever uses is the tool of *blindness.*

In the Old Testament as well as the New, we see the various attacks of Satan, and for the most part, they are all attempting to bring the Christian down by causing them to *sin.* This was what he attempted to accomplish with his massive assault on Job's family and livestock. When that did not work, and Job remained faithful to God, the attack shifted to Job's *person.* Satan was unrelenting, sending one physical attack after another. Poor Job suffered through so many things that we know it was only due to God's grace that he remained free of sin during that time. It was only toward the end of this satanic (yet God-ordained) ordeal, he began to have a pity party, but even in that, he never cursed God. He remained *faithful.*

In the New Testament, we see Satan's frontal assault on Jesus Himself after Satan led Jesus into the wilderness. There Satan tried three different ways to achieve his goal of bringing Christ down through *sinning.* He was unsuccessful, so he left, waiting for another opportunity (cf. Mark 1:13; Luke 4:1-13).

We see how often Satan used the Pharisees and other religious leaders of Christ's day as a constant thorn in the flesh of Jesus Christ. These men were always questioning the Creator, demanding this or that from Him, and always attempting to trap Him with His words. They never succeeded in causing Him to stumble, much less fall.

We are also privy to how Satan worked in the book of Acts, through constant resistance to the gospel and eventual outright hatred toward the man who became the first martyr of the Church, Stephen, then Peter, then Paul, as well as others. We understand the wiles of the devil from the perspective of the frontal assault. We are taught about his warfare against the believer and we learn what to look for in our daily lives.

In short, authentic believers, if they have any training in the Word at all, know a number of things about Satan:

1. *He hates us*
2. *He accuses and condemns us*
3. *He works against us*
4. *He throws his fiery darts at us*
5. *He works to thwart us*
6. *He works to discourage us*
7. *He works to bring us down in sin*
8. *He works to trivialize our testimony*
9. *He works to cause us to bring dishonor to God*

He does these eight things and more, which are all negative and direct in the obvious sense. However, we are too often blind to what Satan does *indirectly*. We focus so much on what he is trying to *get us to do (sin)*, that we fail to see what he does not want us to *know*.

Satan and his minions are so busy attacking us that we wind up constantly being on the *defensive*. It is high time that Christians – in these Last Days – go on the *offensive*. The only way to do that is by knowing and understanding the many blessings we have in Christ.

Chapter 5

On the Offense

C an you imagine a sports team or personality that while playing their particular sport was *always* and only on the defensive end of things and were never trained in offense? How could he know or understand what offensive players might do without this kind of training? While most college and pro sports teams have a defensive and an offensive line or team, each person is aware of the role of the players on both sides.

The practice of separate offensive and defensive teams has not always been though, and when football began (literally, between Ivy League schools), there were hardly any rules and usually the same

guys played both offense and defense. Let's pretend that this is
the way the teams are today.
Every member of each team
plays and understands both offense and defense. Could you
imagine how tiring and defeating
it would be if every time your
team played against another
team, it was always as the *defense*? You could never win, because you could never score.
You never get the ball to keep
once, always giving it up as soon
as you got it, handed it over to
the other team. You would never
get the chance to have one of the players go out for a short pass or a
long bomb. The quarterback would never be allowed to run it up the
middle, or hand it off to someone else to either run it or pass it.

No, your team was *always* trying to keep the other team from getting
into *your* end zone. In fact, the first order of business is *not giving up*
any of your part of the field. Imagine playing the entire game this
way, *every* game.

All of us have seen games where this has happened. Probably one of
the most lopsided victories was in 1990 when the *"San Francisco
49ers faced off against the Denver Broncos in what would become the
most lopsided victory in Superbowl history. The 49ers demolished the
Broncos by a final score of 55-10 to become Superbowl XXIV cham-
pions."*[2] In a game such as that one, the Broncos wound up inadvertently playing defense most of the game.

---

[2] http://football.about.com/library/weekly/aa012400a.htm

Playing that type of game is not only *tiring*, but also emotionally *debilitating* because after a while, it is easy to begin thinking of yourself as a *loser* since you have no opportunity to score. Now compare and contrast this with the 49ers in that same game. Obviously, both of these teams did *well* to get to the Superbowl in the first place, but obviously only one team can *win*. What you do not want to happen if you are the team that loses is to lose by so much!

The 49ers smashed the Broncos, simply playing better at every turn that day. It was a win and a victory that made them feel good. They were victorious! They were the best! No one could take that away from them. It was theirs to keep!

Think of the Broncos though. They were a good team, good enough to get to the Superbowl. Yet, they were not even close (that day), to rivaling, what the 49ers dished out. Because of it, they lost mercilessly. Did they feel good about the way they played? They could not have because they lost so brutally. Wondering what went wrong, all they could do was watch the 49ers celebrate, and view the game videos repeatedly, in the hopes of learning from their mistakes to do better next time.

The interesting thing about playing a sport is that once you begin to realize that you are "on top" of things, it really starts to flow. It normally catches on to the other players as well. Confidence begins to swell and before you know it, you're making passes, catching throws, zigzagging through the line with hardly any effort. That builds more confidence.

At the same time, the other team, sensing your team's confidence, tries harder to keep you either from gaining any yardage, or to bringing you down altogether. Ideally, they want to steal the ball from you before you've had your fourth down. However, because they sense the self-assurance you have, their efforts create problems for *them*. They wind up making careless errors, like stepping over the line before the ball is snapped, or in their exuberance to tackle the ball holder, they wind up getting too much facemask, or hair, or something. In other words, your confidence takes their *confidence* away. While theirs continues to grow, your team becomes more deflated.

Friends, this is exactly what happens in the spiritual realm. Satan does his best to keep us constantly *on guard*, and because of it, we wind up being on the defensive nearly all the time.

We are aware of the fact that believers should strive not to sin, and when we *do* sin, we understand that we need to *confess* that sin, in order that God's forgiveness will be *applied*. What we wind up doing then is to become constantly aware of the pitfalls of sinning and that temptation lurks around every corner.

Being On Guard Is Not All We Can Do

While we may *think* that being *on our guard* is the extent of our ability to be on the *offensive*, I believe that this is only part of it. Our focus is wrong because it is incomplete. We wind up focusing primarily on the fact that at any moment temptation will rear its ugly head from every corner, crack, or crevice. Because of this, and all the energy it takes to be continually aware of that possibility, we spend little time focusing on the benefits and blessings we *have* (present tense) in Christ because of our actual *standing*.

State vs. Standing

A huge difference exists between the authentic Christian's *state* (our *walk* in this life) and his *standing* (our *position* in Christ). Our standing is who we are *in Christ spiritually*, while our state is our *experience* or *walk* in this physical world. It is my contention that the more we comprehend our true *standing in Christ*, the greater the benefit to our *state*. They go hand in hand, which is exactly why our Adversary Satan, prefers to keep us blinded to the facts of our *standing* in Christ and the blessings and benefits associated with it.

Chapter 6

Our State

When we speak of the Christian's *state*, we are referring to his or her *walk* in this physical world; the daily experience of life in this realm. It differs from our *standing* in that our standing refers to what we *are in Christ,* or how God sees us. It is more difficult to wrap our brains around our *standing* in Christ. This is mainly because we do not necessarily *feel* we are different after becoming a Christian (though we might), although many teach that without an accompany feeling, our salvation may be in question. When we read about the various blessings in the Bible that belong to authentic believers (such as the fact that we have been declared *righteous*), since we live with ourselves every day, the failures in our lives make it difficult to understand how God can see us *as righteous.* In other words, it is hard to believe it, because we naturally compare what the Bible says with our daily life and since we live in the *physical realm*, we know what we experience. We know what we *feel*, we know what we *hear*, we know what we *say*, and in general, we are all too familiar with this life of ours because it is literally how our physical body relates and reacts to the life we *live* here on earth. The Holy Spirit wants us to understand that this is merely a *reflection* of the true reality that our soul experiences and what we *will fully experience* one day because of our *standing.* This life is nothing but a vapor, which is here today and gone tomorrow. What is 50, 60, 70, 80 years or more when compared with *eternity*, which never ends? While we tend to think that this life *feels* as if it goes on and on, as we age, we come to know what it means when we hear people talk of life speeding by us.

Thinking Back About Looking Forward

When we were young kids, there was a string of highpoints in life that we longed to reach. Learning to drive and obtaining a driver's license at 16 was certainly one of them. Turning 18 years of age was another, because you were then considered legal adult, which also meant that you could be drafted into the military. Another milestone for too many people is turning twenty-one years of age, because this allows them to drink...*legally.*

After these milestones, things are not generally measured in specific years. They become celebrated *events.* College life came and then went. Looking for a mate to share the remainder of your life with was often considered during that time in college or shortly thereafter. A career choice is often determined as well during this time.

Before it is realized, time has gone by, all of those milestones were reached, and then retirement is here! Wow, where did the time go?

As I write this, in a few days I will be 53 years old. The weirdest thing is that I do not *feel* 53 years old. Oh, sometimes my body tells me that it is that old (or older, depending how much gardening or work around the house I have done), but *inside* my mind, I feel like I am still in my late teens or early twenties. How does *that* happen?

Still, regardless of how many more years the Lord has set aside for me on this planet, once I slip into eternity from this life, I am quite certain that this life will be initially hardly remembered and then forgotten completely, with any tears wiped away as well (Isaiah 25:8). If we *could* measure this life against the coming life for the authentic believer, there is no comparison. No comparison whatsoever.

Mark it well, the more Satan can keep our eyes fixed on *this life*, with all its faults, foibles and *sin*, the more he can keep us from knowing and appreciating that our *standing in Christ* translates to and benefits us in this life. We must *seek to understand it*, and pray that the Holy Spirit will open our eyes to that reality. This only happens as we literally and spiritually, fix our eyes on Jesus, the Author and Perfector of our faith (cf. Hebrews 12:1-2).

I wonder how many of us realize that the Holy Spirit does a number of things, which lead up to and include our salvation, yet these things are not all often understood. We realize of course, that Jesus spoke of the work of the Holy Spirit, who *"will reprove the world of **sin**, and of **righteousness**, and of **judgment**: Of **sin**, because they believe not on me; Of **righteousness**, because I go to my Father, and ye see me no more; Of **judgment**, because the prince of this world is judged,"* (John 16:8b-11; emphasis added).

In the above text, Jesus is speaking to His disciples and tells them that when He leaves this earth, He will send the Holy Spirit. The Holy Spirit then calls people to come to Christ for salvation. He is the one who draws and opens eyes. Chafer comments, *"Evidently, this specific work is wrought in behalf of the* cosmos *world, but, of necessity, it is directed, not to the cosmos as a whole but to the individual.*"[3] The threefold work of the Holy Spirit is noted by the bolded words above. We see then that it is the Spirit's work to convict of *sin, righteousness, and judgment.* Regarding sin, it is understood that people need to come under conviction for it. We understand that this is an important part of realizing our need *for* Christ.

However, consider the second and third bolded words, *righteousness, and judgment.* What does it mean that the Holy Spirit is sent to *convict* of righteousness? That certainly seems odd. Even Christ's own explanation on the surface does not seem to clarify His first sentence. Let's deal with them one at a time, and in order of their mention.

Sin

Sin is that which is against God's will. Anything that God does *not* want us to do, but we do, *is sin.* It is living outside the boundaries of God's will for us. The apostle John refers to it as *lawlessness* (cf. 1 John 3:4). It is not following God's law. The biggest mistake anyone can ever make in this life is a continued failure to *not* believe on Jesus Christ. This involves:

- *Not believing that He is God*
- *Not believing why He came to this earth as a Man*
- *Not believing that His death was a propitiation for us*
- *Not believing that He rose from the dead*
- *Not believing that He ascended to heaven*

We understand that everyone who leaves this life without having repented (changing his or her mind about the above bulleted list) leaves without gaining salvation. In essence then, *a continued state of unbelief until death* is the unpardonable sin. It *rejects* the conviction of the Holy Spirit and grieves God. No one who dies in unbelief will ever have salvation.

---

[3] Lewis Sperry Chafer *Systematic Theology Vol 3* (Kregel Publications, 1948, 1976), 217

Much Crying and Shedding of Tears

In order to be ready to receive salvation, a person *must* come under the convicting power of the Holy Spirit. Nevertheless, what is this conviction from the Holy Spirit? There is unfortunately, a growing movement within Christendom today, which in my view makes repentance something that it is not, according to Scripture.

Many believe that in order to receive authentic salvation, repentance must be seen, it must be heard and it often involves the sights and sounds of real crying, abject sorrow, and even self-reproach. In essence, in order for someone to experience real repentance, it is believed that they must be cut to the heart. In other words, the person coming under conviction of the Holy Spirit *must* be *undone*. They must be brought low, unable to stand up under the pressure of such conviction, as they are so moved to realize their utter inability to save themselves from their own fate, and to see their need for Christ is due to their great and insurmountable sin.

The problem with this view is that it is difficult to find in the Scriptures. In Scripture, we repeatedly read of people who were converted and it is not uncommon to see them exult in joy, not wither in abject sorrow. Whether it was Zacchaeus, the thief on the cross, any of the disciples who became apostles, Paul, the Ethiopian eunuch, the jailer of Acts, or nearly any other person, what we see are people who in some cases receive salvation almost matter-of-factly, while others are elated to have met the living God! While this *may* result in tears, it does not have to. Yet, this is not what we often hear of today. There is a current backlash against what has been termed "easy believism," and rightly so, if in fact it *is* that. However, in the Scriptures, faith, which brings salvation came by hearing, and hearing by the Word of God (cf. Romans 10:17). Apart from this, there seem to be no other requirement.

Easy Believism

What *is* easy believism? To hear some tell it, the idea that all one has to do is *believe* that Jesus died for my sins (*embracing* that truth through belief and salvation is theirs) is too *simple*. They assert that something *else* is required to *show* that salvation has actually occurred. What does the Bible say?

*"That whosoever **believeth** in him should not perish, but have eternal life. For God so loved the world, that he gave his only begotten Son, that whosoever **believeth** in him should not perish, but have everlasting life. For God sent not his Son into the world to condemn the world; but that the world through him might be saved. He that **believeth** on him is **not condemned**: but he that **believeth** not is condemned already, because he hath not **believed** in the name of the only begotten Son of God,"* (John 3:16-18).

What Jesus is saying in the above text is that *whoever <u>believes</u> on Him will not perish*. There is nothing in that entire text above, which speaks of anything a person has to *do* except *believe*. It amounts to trusting in Jesus' redemptive work on our behalf.

This is how Abraham was saved (counted as righteous; Genesis 15), and everyone else in the Old Testament as well as the New. Salvation comes to each person when it is believed that Jesus is *God*, that He lived a sinless life, that He died a horribly brutal death, and that through the shedding of His blood, our sins were forgiven. While on the cross, He endured the wrath of God that was supposed to have been poured out on you and me (and unfortunately *will* be poured out on everyone who refuses to believe on Him). Having died, He rose from the dead because death could not keep Him. This He did for *you* and for me.

In other words, when we believe or place our trust in Jesus Christ, it ultimately means understanding all of the things just mentioned and firmly accepting the work that He did as true. Believing in Christ is *not* intellectual assent. It is not simply saying "*Oh that sounds good. That makes sense to me*," regarding what I have just stated about Jesus Christ and all that He did for us. Some might say that all of this sounds reasonable *for the Christian religion*, but they also might say that it is unreasonable that everyone should accept it as true. They also might say that while they *understand what I am saying*, they may firmly disagree with it. In either of these cases, they have merely given their intellectual assent, but they certainly have not in any way, shape, or form believed on Him whom God has sent.

Salvation is *realizing* these truths, and *embracing* them so that they become a firmly established confidence within the person. It is having your eyes open to that truth so that it becomes *knowledge*, which can then be embraced. Once embraced, it becomes *inner conviction.*

Easy believism is really a misnomer, because it is actually *intellectual assent*, which as we have stated does not necessarily believe anything. There is no such thing as *easy believism*, none whatsoever. When it comes to salvation, God has made it extremely simple, so that we are without excuse. He also made it simple so that it is something that *everyone* can receive. It does *not* require a genius, a prodigy, or a rocket scientist.

Either we *believe* in Jesus Christ's finished work on *our behalf*, or we do not. It must become *personalized* within each individual. Anything less than that is merely *intellectual assent.* This simply means that while a person might *understand* or *agree* with what is being stated, it does not necessarily mean he or she *embraces* it. This is an extremely important difference.

Zane Hodges comments on this area by stating, "*Among the most frequent code words encountered in lordship teaching are those found in expressions like 'cheap grace,' 'easy believism,' and 'intellectual assent.' All three phrases are usually used to disparage the idea that eternal life can be obtained by a simple act of trust in Christ. All three represent a seriously distorted assessment of the issues involved. Naturally the saving grace of God could never be described as 'cheap' in the negative sense this word often has. The fact is that God paid an enormous price – the death of His Son – to make His grace available to us. Simply because the offer is made free of charge to us does not transform that grace into something 'cheap' or valueless."*[4]

What faith really is, in biblical language, is receiving the testimony of God. It is the inward conviction that what God says to us in the gospel is true. That—and that alone—is saving faith."[5]

Is that not what Abraham did when God spoke to him, promising him a variety of things? He *believed* God and because of that simple belief in God's Word, Abraham was counted righteous. In other words, he became *saved*. By the exercise of our faith in God's Word, we are also declared righteous, are we not?

Hodges goes on to refer us to John 6:47, which states, *"Verily, verily, I say unto you, He that believeth on me hath everlasting life."* Hodge comments, *"Yet though the average person, and even a child, can grasp John 6:47, some Christian teachers and theologians do not! In what must certainly be one of the worst distortions of the Bible in our day, the meaning of our Lord's words is radically transformed by those who hold to lordship salvation. From being a model of simplicity, the Savior's statement is reduced to incomprehensible obscurity. What He really meant by these words – so we are told – is something like this:*

> *Most assuredly, I say to you, he who* **repents**, **believes**, *and* **submits** *totally to my will, has everlasting life."*[6] (emphasis added)

Consider the fact that most of us make and receive promises. Let's not consider at this point promises made of a legal nature, such as buying a car, a home, or something else. We are simply considering

---

[4] Zane C. Hodges *Absolutely Free!* (Acadamie Books, 1989), 29
[5] Ibid, 31
[6] Ibid, 26

the fact that with our close friends, we commit ourselves to them, or they to us through one promise or another. Because of this, and our relationship with them, we merely take their word for granted, believing they will accomplish what they have promised to do for us. This truth is important because by simply standing on the fact that when our friend gives us their word that they will do something for us, and we take them at their word, we would not be accused of "easy believism." In fact, it is *because* we so easily and readily believe their word that they are in fact, actually receiving a compliment from us. They have made a commitment, and without the slightest hesitation, we *believe* them. That act of taking them at their word is not only one of the things our friendship with them is built upon, but also it is one of the very things that cause that relationship to grow and deepen. It becomes a confidence within us that their word will be followed by the appropriate promised action.

It seems straightforward enough, does it not? Even in Christ's discussion with Nicodemus (cf. John 3), Christ explained that what must occur in each person's life is to be born from above (of water and spirit). This being born again is predicated *only* on *believing in Jesus.* What has happened is that in an effort to ensure that people are *truly* saved (as if anyone but God would actually *know* that!), well meaning individuals have placed their own *additional* requirements on salvation. In their efforts to make the conversion experience more sincere, they have actually made it more difficult. In essence, many of these people believe that it has to pass the muster *externally* and if people are not brought down to the ground in a heap of blubbering puddle, then their conversion experience is questionable.

Demagoguery?
Normally, *repentance* is heavily hammered home to the individual, so that they are aware that coming to Christ and receiving His salvation, is *more* than simply *believing.* While receiving salvation without doubt incorporates a *change* within the life of the person *receiving*

salvation, many of these folks want to see an *outward* change, which they believe is evidence of a true *inward* change. This seems to be a form of demagoguery because they are placing *themselves* in the position of determining who is truly saved and who is not. While an outward reaction *may* be the case for some, it does not always follow that conversion to Christianity is preceded by great sorrow for committed sin, which is often described as true *repentance*. In fact, repentance, in its simplest sense, means to *change one's mind about something*. Whether well meaning or not, *have* these folks actually wound up inadvertently *adding* to the necessary requirement for salvation? Unfortunately, I believe they have done exactly that. While the conversion experience *does* result in a changed life, it becomes problematic when people decide what that change should *look* like in each conversion.

Of course, the best place to observe examples of individuals who received salvation is the Bible itself. What did their conversion *look* like to those around them and what was it that prompted Christ to pronounce, in some way, that they had in fact *received* salvation? We know that as far as the Old Testament is concerned, the *same* faith was required to gain salvation, (which included being declared righteous, as in the case of Abraham). What about the New Testament?

Zacchaeus

Zacchaeus is a well-known biblical character, which we have read about numerous times in the gospel of Luke 17:1-10 (emphasis below, added).

"And Jesus entered and passed through Jericho. And, behold, there was a man named Zacchaeus, which was the chief among the publicans, and he was rich. And he sought to see Jesus who he was; and could not for the press, because he was little of stature. And he ran before, and climbed up into a sycamore tree to see him: for he was to pass that way. And when Jesus came to the place, he looked up, and saw him, and said unto him, Zacchaeus, make haste, and come down; for to day I

*must abide at thy house. And he made haste, and came down, and received him joyfully. And when they saw it, they all murmured, saying, That he was gone to be guest with a man that is a sinner. And Zacchaeus stood, and said unto the Lord: Behold, Lord, the half of my goods I give to the poor; and if I have taken any thing from any man by false accusation, I restore him fourfold. And Jesus said unto him, **This day is salvation come to this house**, forsomuch as he also is a son of Abraham. For the Son of man is come to seek and to save that which was lost."*

If we consider the narrative carefully, here is what we learn in the order in which it occurred:

1. *Christ came to Jericho*
2. *Zacchaeus lived in Jericho and had obviously heard about the ministry of Jesus*
3. *Being short, in order to see Jesus as He passed by, Zacchaeus had to climb a tree to see over the crowd (many of us can relate to that problem!)*
4. *As Jesus passed by, He noticed Zacchaeus and told him that He was supposed to stay at Zacchaeus' house that day*
5. *Zacchaeus quickly descended to the ground*
6. *Zacchaeus received Jesus "joyfully"*
7. *The crowd murmured against Jesus because He was willing to stay at the home of a "sinner."*
8. *Zacchaeus quickly diffused the situation by stating that he promised to give half of his goods to the poor*
9. *Zacchaeus also stated that if he had cheated anyone, he would restore to that individual "fourfold."*
10. *Jesus replies that salvation had come that day to Zacchaeus' house.*

It seems clear enough, doesn't it? Jesus was literally saying that Zacchaeus *had received salvation.* How can anyone argue with that?

There is nothing in the narrative that indicates any of the following existed or was in evidence **prior** to Zacchaeus receiving salvation:

- *A repentant demeanor (sad, morose, self-denigrating, tears, etc.)*
- *A promise to give away half his goods to the poor*
- *A promise to restore fourfold to anyone whom he may have cheated*
- *Praying the "sinner's prayer"*

None of the above is seen in the narrative *before* Zacchaeus received salvation from our Lord and some of it is not in any part of the narrative. What we *do* see prior to his receiving salvation is:

- *An anxious curiosity or interest in Jesus*
- *A strong desire to be near Jesus*
- *Not allowing his lack of height to keep him from seeing Jesus as He walked by*

If we are not careful, as we read the narrative, we may also miss the fact that as soon as Jesus called to Zacchaeus, he responded *quickly* and *joyfully.*

Again, are some people guilty of making the conversion experience more difficult than the simplicity of Jesus' explanation? At the same time, are other guilty of creating a process of receiving salvation, which is not biblically based? It certainly appears that the only thing required of Zacchaeus for salvation was to *believe* on Jesus. The change that occurred *within* Zacchaeus *after* he had *received salvation* was the very thing that *prompted* him to want to *prove* that his conversion was *real*, *actual*, *authentic*, and *true*. This change of heart took place within Zacchaeus *because* of the salvation he had just received. It did not come about by confessing his multitude of sins, nor did it come about by praying a certain prayer. It came about because of Zacchaeus' change in attitude toward Christ and trust in Him.

In the narrative, there is no indication of *tears*, *self-condemnation*, *self-denigration*, or *self-castigation*. Zacchaeus' repentance consisted of *changing his mind about Jesus* and what He came to accomplish for humanity. We do not know when this change actually took place. What we know is that Jesus was able to point out the fact that salvation had come to Zacchaeus based upon Zacchaeus' declaration to Jesus afterwards. This change is the result of the Holy Spirit's quickening. Note again that Zacchaeus received it with *joy*.

The Thief on the Cross
The story of the thief is found in Luke 23. You will recall that the scene is during Christ's crucifixion, and one could say that the thief is a minor character, yet an important one. He is important not only because as a valuable human being, he has salvation and is with God now, but also because the situation proves God's *love* for the sinner, even to the point of giving this dying man (the thief), one final chance to receive that salvation.

• *A Brief Aside – God's Love*
Speaking of God's love, this would be a good time to define it, especially in this day and age when God's love has virtually been reduced to rank sentimentality.

Recently, as I was researching on the 'Net, I came across a site in which these words were stated, "*It certainly is **not** true that 'God hates the sin but loves the sinner,' as commonly preached by false teachers. This phrase is not in the Bible. Sin is never separated from the sinner as if it were an independent entity. People are never separated from their sin as if they were independent from their sin.*"[7] (emphasis added)

Not far down on the same page, we read the words, "*God is love and His love endures forever. We are to love one another as God has loved*

---

[7] http://www.biblelife.org/attributes.htm

us. We must keep in mind to whom these verses were written [verses were listed – ed.]. **They were written to the believer and instruct us in our attitude and actions toward other believers**."[8] (emphasis added)

The verses the individual quoted *do* reference believers, but what that individual is forgetting (or possibly ignoring), are the Beatitudes and the Sermon on the Mount, which we will go into shortly. If the above quote is true, then our *only* obligation is to love other believers. *Is it?* We will see if he is correct.

Not in the Bible?
Not much further down, the person shares this insight, "'*Unconditional Love' are two words that do not appear together in the Bible, but the concept or doctrine is taught by many pastors. One minister has made the "unconditional love of God" his central theme in books, lessons, tapes, and videos that are targeted for sale to pastors. There is one big problem with the doctrine of God's 'unconditional love.' The doctrine is not in the Bible. The word "unconditional" does not appear in the Bible --- not even once. It is false teaching that originated in the false doctrines of John Calvin. The minister spreading this false doctrine is a rank Calvinist.*"[9]

There are a number of problems with these comments, in my opinion. First, just because specific words or phrases do not actually *appear* in the Bible does not mean that the concept is not *taught* there. For instance, the following words or phrases do not appear in the Bible, but *are* actual doctrines, or concepts gained from Bible study:

- *Trinity*
- *Rapture*

---

[8] http://www.biblelife.org/attributes.htm
[9] Ibid

- *Sunday School*
- *Fundamental*
- *Fundamentalism*
- *Systematic Theology*
- *Theology*
- *Soteriology*
- *Bibliology*
- *Christology*
- *Pneumatology*
- *Eschatology*

You get the point, and you could undoubtedly add your own list of words or phrases to the above list. Simply because a word or phrase does not appear in Scripture, does not mean that the concept it represents is *not* legitimate, as the above examples show.

In fact, the person I have been quoting indicates he believes in the PreTrib Rapture and many argue that the word does not appear in the Bible, so it makes it a false teaching. Obviously, the Rapture has been named such based on the transliteration of the Greek verbiage when Paul used the term "catching, or caught away" in reference to believers (cf. 1 Thessalonians 4:17).

People continually point to the *absence* of a word or phrase in an attempt to prove their position. However, even when a word *is* used in Scripture, like "dispensation," people argue about its ultimate meaning. This argument is not much of an argument at all.

God Hates *and* Loves *Perfectly*
Second, God *does* hate certain things ("*Jacob have I loved, Esau have I hated,*" cf. Malachi 1:2b-3a; Romans 9:13). The very first thing we need to ask ourselves though is this: "*Do I love as <u>God</u> loves, and do I <u>hate</u> as God hates?*" Moreover, when I use the terms *love* and *hate,* do they mean something different from what God means by their usage? While it is often extremely easy for a person to hate someone else

(which is exactly why Jesus warns, "*That whosoever is angry with his brother without a cause shall be in danger of the judgment*"), it is impossible for people to *love and hate as God loves* and *hates*. We love and hate as imperfect sinners, regardless of our saved state. Authentic Christians certainly have a leg up on unbelievers when it comes to loving others, yet the Christian's love is far from perfect. Our hatred is also far from perfect, because while God *does* hate, this action on His part reveals His holiness and perfection, but does not change the fact that *God is love*.

We are also familiar with John 3:16, which clearly states "*For God so loved the world, that he gave his only begotten Son, that whosoever believeth in him should not perish, but have everlasting life.*" God's love for the world (or the people *in* the world) is robust and it is real. He would not have gone through the trouble of being born as a Man (while retaining His complete deity), lived among us for roughly thirty years without sin, *died* for humanity in an unbearably brutal and bloody way, then rose again if He did *not love people*.

D. A. Carson said, "*The difference between us and God in regard to loving and hating is vast. Even as Christians, we remain imperfect in our humanity and cannot love perfectly, nor can we hate perfectly (in other words, without malice). But God can do both of these perfectly, because He is God. God can hate without any sinful intent. Therefore, He can hate the sin and the sinner in a perfectly holy way and still be willing to lovingly forgive at the moment of that sinner's repentance and faith (Malachi 1:3; Revelation 2:6; 2 Peter 3:9).*"[10]

Carson goes on to say, "*The Bible clearly teaches that God is love. First John 4:8-9 says, "Whoever does not love does not know God, because God is love. This is how God showed his love among us: He sent his one and only Son into the world that we might live through him." Mysterious but true is the fact that God can perfectly love and hate a person*

---

[10] D. A. Carson *The Difficult Doctrine of the Love of God* (Crossway Books, 1999)

at the same time. This means He can love him as someone He created and can redeem, as well as hate him for his unbelief and sinful lifestyle. We, as imperfect human beings, cannot do this; thus, we must remind ourselves to 'love the sinner, hate the sin.'

"How exactly does that work? We hate sin by refusing to take part in it and by condemning it when we see it. Sin is to be hated, not excused or taken lightly. We love sinners by being faithful in witnessing to them of the forgiveness that is available through Jesus Christ. A true act of love is treating someone with respect and kindness even though he/she knows you do not approve of his lifestyle and/or choices. It is not loving to allow a person to remain stuck in sin. It is not hateful to tell a person he/she is in sin. In fact, the exact opposites are true. We love the sinner by speaking the truth in love. We hate the sin by refusing to condone, ignore, or excuse it."

Along those lines, we also love sinners by never taking vengeance on things they may do to us. Instead, we turn these situations over to the Lord because we know and understand that they did not happen to us by accident, but because the Lord Himself either allowed or directed events to occur in our lives.

Chapter 7

How Are We to Love?

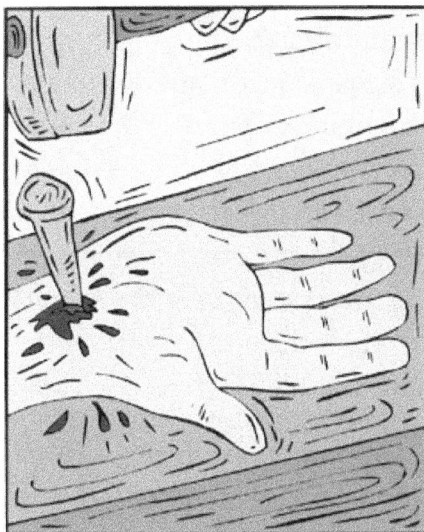

It is far better for Christians to *love people* than try to come up with the perfect way to *hate* them and their sin, yet still be willing to *evangelize* them. If we hate the sinner as well as their sin, yet we still seek to evangelize them, what is that? Jonah fell into that category, did he not? When God told him to go to Nineveh, he *ran the other way*. Why? Because he *knew* that preaching to the people of Nineveh would result in their repentance (cf. Jonah 4).

We would *never* be able to do this in this life; not in a million years. Only God is able to perfectly hate sin and sinners, yet love them enough to be willing to die for them. That seems like a contradiction, which only proves that it is impossible for human beings to hate *and* love as God hates and loves.

The Greatest Commandment?

We read in Matthew's gospel Jesus' answer to a young man who inquired about which commandment was the greatest. *"Master, which is the great commandment in the law? Jesus said unto him, Thou shalt love the Lord thy God with all thy heart, and with all thy soul, and with all thy mind. This is the first and great commandment. **And the second is like unto it, Thou shalt love thy neighbour as thyself**. On these two commandments hang all the law and the prophets,"* (Matthew 22:36-40; emphasis added).

In Matthew 5, Jesus said something even more astonishing. *"Ye have heard that it hath been said, Thou shalt love thy neighbour, and hate thine enemy. But I say unto you, **Love your enemies, bless them that curse you, do good to them that hate you, and pray for them which despitefully use you, and persecute you**,"* (Matthew 5:43-44; emphasis added).

It seems clear that we are to love *all* people, doing good things for all. If we try to do good *to* and *for* those who are unsaved, yet we do it grudgingly (or with annoyance, or even hatred), our actions will seem completely shallow to them and for good reason. We are to love all, especially those of the household of God (cf. Galatians 6:10). However, in what way are we to truly love our neighbors *and* God?

Not long ago, I was having a religious discussion with some folks on a forum (something I generally try to avoid). The subject of homosexuality came up and of course with it, the debate about whether one can be an authentic believer *and* a practicing homosexual. We went back and forth and the person I was ultimately debating with (who indicated she *was* a Christian), came prepared with all the propaganda heard within the ranks of Gay groups who not only want the world to believe that they are Christians, but that their lifestyles are accepted by God.

The discussion turned to Sodom and Gomorrah and the "*real*" reason God decided to shower it with fire and brimstone. The individual just referred to indicated, "*If one reads the story of Sodom and Gomorrah in translations done from the Hebrew, the sin was one of trying to force alien customs on people who found them abhorrent.*" This type of textual rigmarole is not only obvious, but also demeaning to those of us trying to have a serious conversation.

I pointed out that God's decision to destroy Sodom and Gomorrah came *before* the two men (angels) entered the town and were nearly set upon by the homosexual men of the town. In other words, this event (that almost all point to and those within the Gay community do their level best to explain away), had absolutely no bearing on God's decision to destroy the towns. He had *already* made that decision!

Friendship Evangelism

We then segued into a discussion of God's love and how we should love people. The same person I just quoted indicated that rather than "judge" people (especially homosexuals), she believed God would have her *befriend* them and *pray* for them, rather than praying for them *and* witnessing to them.

Funny, I do not recall that as being part of Jesus' mode of operation when it came to evangelism. He did not worry about befriending people. He was infinitely more concerned about their understanding of their own sinful condition, so that they could hopefully see Him as the solution.

Of course, during the conversation, the subject of loving people continued to come up. We must love people, not judge them, etc. I finally said that if we truly LOVE people as God loves people and if we are desirous of showing God how much we love HIM, then we will tell people about their need for salvation! It is that simple. If we truly love people, we will *tell them about Jesus* and let the chips fall where they may fall. We cannot hide behind the *"Oh, I don't want to judge people, so I will just be friends with them and pray that God will be able to tell them about Himself through my life's witness."* What witness? You are there, having befriended the *lost* of this world and all you are doing is *praying* for them?

If we love God, we will keep His commandments. His most important commandment was to go into the entire world and preach the gospel to every creature, (cf. Mark 15:16). There is no better way to show God *and* our neighbor how much we love them. IF we love them, we will *tell* them the Good News – Jesus came, died, and rose again in order that we might have life eternal.

What better gift could we give anyone than that? No greater gift that can be given to anyone. certainly, we are to feed the hungry, clothe the naked and in general meet the needs of people *where we can*, but all of that should lead to giving them the gift that surpasses all other gifts and keeps on giving for all eternity: knowledge of salvation.

This is how we love people. We are not to hate the sinner; we are to love the sinner by introducing them to the only One who can save them for all eternity. We tell them *because* we love them. Humankind is worth saving. Obviously, God thinks so, and He tells us to think so as well.

Francis A. Schaeffer has said, *"All men bear the image of God. They have value, not because they are redeemed, but because they are God's creation in God's image. Modern man, who has rejected this, has no clue as to who he is, and because of this he can find no real value for himself or for other men. Hence, he downgrades the value of other men and produces the horrible thing we face today — a sick culture in which men treat men as inhuman, as machines. As Christians, however, we know the value of men."*[11]

It is difficult to understand where people get the idea that Christians are to *hate the sinner*. If *God* chooses to do that, or does that because it is part of His nature, fine. He is the only One who has the capacity to do that and remain *holy*. Can we? No.

It seems to me that the Christian who hates the sin *and* the sinner needs to condemn themselves as well since the Christian is never completely free from sin in this life. Yet, even if we could get to a point of being sinless, it is only because God would have gotten us there. Nothing we do is going to bring this about, because our sin nature remains with us.

D. A. Caron explains this concept in more depth. *"One evangelical cliché has it that God hates the sin but loves the sinner. There is a small element of truth in these words: God has nothing but hate for the sin, but it would be wrong to conclude that God has nothing but hate for the sinner. A difference must be maintained between God's view of sin and his view of the sinner. Nevertheless the cliché...is false on the face of it and should be abandoned."*[12]

The truth seems to be that we tend to view God's wrath and love similar to our own versions of love and wrath. However, since our wrath and love are not like God's love and wrath, and as Carson states in another paragraph of his book, neither His wrath or His love stem from a type of blind rage, which ultimately control Him, but instead

---

[11] Francis A. Schaeffer *The Mark of the Christian* (InterVarsity Press; 1970), 9
[12] D. A. Carson *The Difficult Doctrine of the Love of God* (Crossways Books; 2000), 68-69

flow from His own nature, in perfect harmony with all that He is, as God.[13]

I believe God can be *both* loving toward those of this world, who are ultimately, rebellious and lawless, and wrathful toward the same. If not, then what does it mean when we read in Scripture that God loved the world enough to send His Son into it, not to condemn it, but for the purposes of redemption? (cf. John 3)

Returning to the Thief

The text from each of the gospel accounts concerning the thief on the cross is included below. The most detailed account is Luke's gospel. Both Matthew and Mark note two thieves, saying they both ridiculed Jesus. The gospel of John states there were two thieves who died with Jesus, one on either side of Him.

While some might be tempted to point out what they believe to be an obvious contradiction, no such contradiction exists. It is clear from the context of each gospel that each writer emphasized different aspects of Jesus Christ. Because three of the accounts provide us with knowledge that there were *two* thieves, and in two of those narratives (Matthew and Mark), we learn that *both* cast aspersions on Jesus Christ, it is safe to *assume* that this same thing occurred in Luke's account. However, rather than focus on the two thieves both chiding and ridiculing Christ, Luke reports what happened *after* that when one of the thieves came to the realization of who Jesus was, as He hung on the cross next to Him.

"And one of the malefactors which were hanged railed on him, saying, If thou be Christ, save thyself and us. But the other answering rebuked him, saying, Dost not thou fear God, seeing thou art in the same condemnation? And we indeed justly; for we receive the due reward of our deeds: but this man hath done nothing amiss. And he said unto Jesus,

---

[13] D. A. Carson *The Difficult Doctrine of the Love of God* (Crossways Books; 2000), 69

Lord, remember me when thou comest into thy kingdom. And Jesus said unto him, Verily I say unto thee, Today shalt thou be with me in paradise," (Luke 23:39-43)

"The thieves also, which were crucified with him, cast the same in his teeth," (Matthew 27:44).

"And they that were crucified with him reviled him," (Mark 15:32)

"Where they crucified him, and two other with him, on either side one, and Jesus in the midst," (John 19:18)

Please give attention specifically to Luke's narrative account. All accounts taken together force us to conclude that both thieves gave Jesus a hard time about His death and why was He not able to save Himself *from* that death. As noted, Luke seems to pay attention only to the one thief who *changed his mind* about Jesus.

The Thief's Demeanor

Note carefully that in Luke's entire narrative regarding this thief, not once do we read where the thief cried, or is said to have given evidence of deep internal remorse. What seems to have transpired is the opening of his eyes to the truth of Jesus Christ, His Person and His mission to humanity. This could have only been done by the Holy Spirit, where at one point, the thief was completely blind to the truth of Jesus, and the next was perfectly able to see His true identity. This only comes through the ministry of the Holy Spirit and none other.

Had the thief called out for *forgiveness*, had he been filled with *self-remonstration* for his lawlessness, had he come face to face with *himself* in all of his sinful shame, we can be assured that at least *one* of the gospel writers would have recorded that for us. However, we see *none* of it. Instead we witness a man, who at the end of his life, was blessed enough to have the *eyes of his understanding opened* in order that he might *believe*. It is clear that he *did* believe because of what he *says* to Jesus. With conviction, he *embraced* the truth that had been revealed to Him.

"*Lord, remember me when thou comest into thy kingdom,*" was what the thief asked for, and not only was it granted, but the thief received more than he could have ever hoped! He was given eternal life, and that very day he would begin to see it in paradise! He had come to understand that Jesus was indeed a *King*!

The fact that the thief asked Jesus to remember him *when He came into His Kingdom* shows us that he at once understood who Jesus was, as he hung there next to him. Was it the placard above Jesus' head telling the world that that Man who was dying *was* the King of the Jews? Possibly. We are not told *what* the Holy Spirit used to open the man's eyes. Nevertheless, we see the *results* of the man's eyes having been opened. He *believed* on Jesus Christ. It is realized that there are some who do not believe this man was actually saved at all. They have their ways of explaining what they believe transpired. They are entitled to their opinion. For us, there is no doubt that the thief received *salvation* as he hung on the cross, just as Zacchaeus received it also.

Numerous Examples

There are many instances of people receiving the Lord's salvation in the New Testament. For example, in Acts (also penned by Luke), chapter eleven, we read of God's vision to Peter. He was shown a great sheet holding all types of beasts and God told him to kill and eat. Peter of course, having been raised Jewish probably thought it was a test and said that he could not eat anything because Mosaic Law did not allow many of these particular animals to be eaten food. God gave the same vision to Peter a second time and said that he (Peter) should not label something *unclean* that God has called clean. The purpose of this vision was not to change Peter's eating habits. It was for what was to come next in his life, which was his calling to Gentiles.

Cornelius sent men to bring Peter to him so that he could hear more about Jesus. Unfortunately, Cornelius was *Gentile*, which meant that an orthodox Jew would not be able to go into a Gentile's house if he could help it because it meant that he would become unclean. For an orthodox Jew to become clean once again required seven days of rituals. However, it is also plain from the text that God had already begun a work in Peter *prior* to receiving this vision. In verse six of chapter ten, we read that Peter was staying with someone named *"Simon a tanner, whose house is by the sea side."* Did you get that? Simon, a tanner, had a business in which touching dead animals was part of his normal day. Yet, it was unlawful for a Jew to be in a person's house where dead animals were, much less touch a dead animal. However, here is where Peter was staying, in the house of someone who routinely dealt with dead things, which if Peter had been concerned, he knew his very presence there would have made him unclean.

Fresh from the vision, these men appear at Peter's door and because of that vision, he knew he was to go to Cornelius' house, which he did. When he got there, he preached the gospel of Jesus Christ and salvation was received. However, note in Acts 11:2-3, after Peter returned to Jerusalem. *"And when Peter was come up to Jerusalem, they that were of the circumcision contended with him, Saying, Thou wentest in to men uncircumcised, and didst eat with them."* Uh oh, there is going to be trouble in River City because Peter did what good Jews did not do.

I like what Hodges says regarding this situation, *"Does this sound familiar? This was precisely the criticism that the scribes and Pharisees made about Jesus Himself. It was also the spirit of the elder brother of the prodigal son. In fact, in the concluding section of our Lord's narrative in Luke 15, the father of the repentant boy goes out to the older brother to invite him to the banquet inside. But the self-righteous older brother rudely rejects the opportunity for fellowship with his father and with his younger brother.*"[14]

Referring to verse 18 of Acts 11, Peter has explained the entire situation to his believing brothers in Jerusalem who questioned him going inside a Gentile's home. Not only did they *not* act like the older brother, but they also changed their attitude! "*When they heard these things, they held their peace, and glorified God, saying, Then hath God also to the Gentiles granted repentance unto life.*"

Hodges comments here are also noteworthy. "*Let these words not be misread. Emphatically they do* not *say, 'repentance unto eternal life.' Instead, they are the reflection of that 'coming to life' which is always the end result of repentance whether it be the repentance of a Christian or the repentance of the unsaved.*"[15]

What Hodges is saying here is that the brothers who *changed* their opinion and realized that the Gentiles were also granted "repentance unto life," meant that their eyes opened to the truth that the gospel of Jesus Christ was also now going out to the Gentiles, separate from the nation of Israel. Cornelius and his household *believed* the truth that Peter taught them. They embraced this revealed truth and this is what occurs when someone *repents*. Because they were enabled to believe Peter and agree with him, they repented of their own error, embracing the truth surrounding Jesus Christ, His life, death, and resurrection. Cornelius and his household became new creations in Christ.

Just the same way, the brothers back in Jerusalem also embraced this truth and because of it, they *continued* to live in the Spirit. Hodges points to Romans 8:13, which says "*For if ye live after the flesh, ye shall die: but if ye through the Spirit do mortify the deeds of the body, ye shall live.*" This is exactly what the Christian leaders in the Jerusalem church *did*. The Holy Spirit opened their eyes to the truth re-

---

[14] Zane C. Hodges *Absolutely Free!* (Acadamie Books, 1989), 153
[15] Ibid, 153

garding Gentiles and salvation, and they **joyfully** *embraced it*! If we consider the salvation that came to Cornelius and his house, we have to note how *quickly* it came to them, with very little effort and with joy, not sorrow.

It's in the *Believing* (Inner Conviction)

There are other instances of people being told to simply *believe* on the Lord Jesus Christ for salvation. The jailer of Thyatira came to the point of asking Paul and Silas, "*Sirs, what must I do to be saved*?"(cf. Acts 16:30b. We will remember that the reason Paul and Silas were in jail to begin with was due to the exorcism Paul performed on a young woman who was known for her *soothsaying* or fortune telling. She began following Paul and Silas around turning into their own personal carnival barker! This grieved Paul because in essence what the demon within the woman was doing was calling attention to Paul and Silas, even though she mentioned "the most high God," (v. 17). This detracted from God's purposes and glory.

Once free of the demon, the woman was unable to tell fortunes and because of this, her master/owner lost a valuable source of income. Since neither Paul nor Silas had money to be able to pay either the man, or the city, they were thrown into jail. However, rather than allow themselves to become depressed over their situation, they chose to deliberately turn a bad situation into good by singing hymns and praise to God (v. 25). They chose to believe that God had a purpose in their incarceration, and in a short while, they would witness it. So they began to sing praises to God *for* the situation.

It was because of their trust in God, that an earthquake occurred, freeing not only Paul and Silas, but also every other prisoner, leaving the doors to each cell wide open! Yet, not one prisoner tried to escape! When the jailer came into the prison and noticed all the doors open, he was not only amazed, but also petrified. He was about ready to fall on his sword simply because he knew that when prisoners escape, the jailer automatically receives a death sentence. Paul stopped him by telling him that all the prisoners were still there.

Something supernatural had occurred and the jailer had not missed it. This caused him to ask question, "*Sirs, what must I do to be saved?*" Some have argued that he was concerned about his *physical* safety because as stated, for a prison chief to lose any prisoners in his prison meant certain execution. This obviously cannot be the case since he asked the question *after* he learned that not one prisoner had left. He would not be put to death or even chastised, since all the prisoners were still there in their cells.

We can safely assume that the man was at that point concerned about *eternity*. He knew that for the prisoners not to have escaped after such an opportune event (the earthquake), was beyond the *physical*. He had also likely heard Paul and Silas singing praises to God, since it was common for the jailer to live right next to or above the jail. This allowed him to get to the jail in a very short space of time and allowed him the ability to keep an eye on things from close proximity. The jailer had also felt the huge earthquake, witnessing its effects, and at once was concerned about escaping prisoners.

When he arrived to the actual jail, and was assured that everyone was still in their cell, he knew at once that what had happened must have been supernatural! Why else would prisoners who were literally free to go, *stay where they were in their own cells*? That is unheard of!

The answer to the jailer's question is found in Acts 16:31, in which we read that both Paul and Silas tell the jailer, "*And they said, Believe on the Lord Jesus Christ, and thou shalt be saved, and thy house.*"

Verse 32 tells us that Paul and Silas explained about Jesus Christ to the jailer and his household. Not long after this, the jailer and his house were baptized then (after he personally cleaned Paul's and Silas' wounds from their beating). Nowhere is there a hint of anyone praying the sinner's prayer, nor does the narrative indicate that either the jailer or anyone in his house was so filled with remorse or self-condemnation. In fact, it appears to be a joyful event.

Returning to Cornelius for a moment, look how quickly salvation is received by Cornelius and his household. "***While Peter yet spake these words, the Holy Ghost fell on all them which heard the word***. *And they of the circumcision which believed were astonished, as many as came with Peter, because that on the Gentiles also was poured out the gift of the Holy Ghost. For they heard them speak with tongues, and magnify God. Then answered Peter, Can any man forbid water, that these should not be baptized, which have received the Holy Ghost as well as we? And he commanded them to be baptized in the name of the Lord. Then prayed they him to tarry certain days*," (Acts 10:44-48; emphasis added).

Note that *while Peter was still speaking*, the Holy Ghost fell on those who were gathered. There is no way to have the Holy Ghost fall on someone and prompt them to speak in unknown tongues, *unless they had received salvation*. It is clear from this example at least that salvation and the pouring out of the Holy Spirit happened *simultaneously* and with no sign of what many today call "repentance." There is no indication of anyone rending their clothes, or sitting in sackcloth and ashes in deep repentance. The narrative does not describe rivers of tears or self-condemnation. There is no "sinner's prayer" being prayed by them. Cornelius and his household had their eyes opened and they *believed* and this occurred while *Peter was still speaking!*

Declared Righteous
We know that an authentic believer is declared righteous and we can be assured that in each of the previous situations, those who became saved, were also declared righteous by God. Because we are righteous, we are then justified and ultimately glorified (cf. Romans 8:30). This is part and parcel of being born again. It comes with

God's package of salvation. Zacchaeus, the thief, the jailer, and Cornelius and his household were all declared righteous the very moment of having received salvation.

Commenting on this righteousness, Chafer notes, *"Since imputed righteousness is the only form of righteousness included in salvation by grace and since this context presents only those most vital truths related to man's salvation which the Holy Spirit reveals, it is clear that the reference here [John 3:18] is to imputed righteousness – that perfect righteousness of God which Christ is and which the believer becomes when in Christ. The whole issue is of a perfect standing before God – far more, indeed, than the removal of sin by forgiveness. It is that which God bestows on 'him that worketh not' (Rom. 4:5)."*[16]

By receiving salvation, we are removed from under God's condemnation *forever* (cf. Romans 8:1). It also forever declares us righteous because of the fact that it is Christ's righteousness, which has been imputed to us (cf. Romans 4:5-6; 22-24; 2 Corinthians 5:21).

In all the previous examples given, there is no indication from those who heard and were changed by the message preached that they were supposed to do something *other* than simply *believe,* or that their sin was brought before them in an inordinate way. To truly *believe* (or *to actively have confidence in*), is an ability which God *grants* based on the truth that person hears and understands. To believe is to *be able to trust* in God the Son; that His atonement on our behalf is vicarious. It is because of His sacrificial death of Jesus that salvation is offered. Do you believe that? Do you have *faith* in that? Do you *trust* in Christ's work on your behalf? Is it more than head knowledge? Is it true in your heart? This is *not* intellectual assent, or easy believism, nor is it *cheap grace.* *"What faith really is, in biblical language, is receiving the testimony of God. It is the* inward conviction

---

[16] Lewis Sperry Chafer *Systematic Theology Vol 3* (Kregel Publications, 1948, 1976), 219

that what God says to us in the gospel is true. That – and that alone – is saving faith."[17]

Regarding these events and the lack of the individual's recognition of sin, Chafer points out, "*it is noticeable, though contrary to general opinion, that the Spirit does not enlighten the mind with respect to all the sins the individual has committed. **It is not a matter of creating shame or remorse concerning sin, nor is it so much as a reminder of sin that has been committed** – though there is nothing, on the other hand, to preclude sorrow or consciousness of sin; it is rather that, since sin has been borne by Christ, there remains the one great and only responsibility of one's attitude toward the Savior who bore the sin. This unbelief the Lord declared is the basis of final condemnation, when He said: 'He that believeth on him is not condemned: but he that believed not is condemned already, because he hate not believed in the name of the only begotten Son of God' (John 3:18)."*[18] (emphasis added)

Even in Peter's sermon recorded for us in Acts 2, the emphasis is not on sin, but on believing in Christ for salvation. What we instead see is Peter's reference to Joel and the last days. Beyond this, we note Peter's declaration about salvation: "*And it shall come to pass, that whosoever shall **call on the name of the Lord** shall be saved,*" (Acts 2:21; emphasis added). Then beginning in verse 22, Peter explains who Jesus was, what He came to do, and how His life was prophesied by David (cf. Acts 2:23-36). Peter points out their sin and rebellion in verse 36, which states, "*Therefore let all the house of Israel know assuredly, that God hath made that same Jesus, whom ye have crucified, both Lord and Christ.*"

Peter was not pointing out the crucifixion to affix blame necessarily (although all people share in that blame). Peter was reminding them

---

[17] Zane C. Hodges *Absolutely Free!* (Acadamie Books, 1989), 31
[18] Lewis Sperry Chafer *Systematic Theology Vol 3* (Kregel Publications, 1948, 1976), 218

of Jesus whom they crucified was very *God* – Lord and Christ. It is this truth that convicts by the Holy Spirit. Peter had spent some time explaining that what David had spoken of could not have been related to himself, but to another. David had not ascended into the heavens, but Jesus had.

What was the reaction of this very first sermon preached by one of Jesus' apostles? *"Now when they heard this, **they were pricked in their heart**, and said unto Peter and to the rest of the apostles, Men and brethren, **what shall we do?**"* (Acts 2:37; emphasis added)

The answer, as given by Peter was *"Then Peter said unto them, Repent, and be baptized every one of you in the name of Jesus Christ for the remission of sins, and ye shall receive the gift of the Holy Ghost,"* (Acts 2:38). Peter told them that they needed to *repent*, which they had actually already done because they were "pricked in their hearts." This led them to *change their mind about Jesus Christ*, who He was and what He accomplished for them. Peter also said that they should be baptized. There is much controversy over this, but I believe that Peter's command to them to be baptized was meant to be nothing more than a clear break with Judaism. Once a Jew was publicly water baptized, this signaled he had embraced another religion, and was *renouncing* Judaism. It also signifies of course, our testimony that we are breaking free with our past and embracing the new creation within us, though it is not dependent upon our salvation.

Two Extremes in Preaching

Yet what is often preached today? Unfortunately, the emphasis is on one or two extremes. Some pulpits will not touch the word "sin" while others want to focus on sin and remorse. Neither allows the Christian to **live** the truth of his or her standing in Christ. *"Gospel preaching has made much of the remission of sin through the redemption that is in Christ Jesus, and not more than should be; **but a deplorable neglect has been accorded the equally requisite truth that a perfect standing is imputed also to the one who believes**. The truth* *of the gospel, as outlined in John 16:7-11, is presented in a full-orbed perfection."*[19] (emphasis added)

Because we are so well versed in sinning and not forgiving as the Lord forgives us, it makes sense that it *seems* more expedient to focus on our sin, our need for *repentance*, and our *lack* of love. In reality, it is merely *easier* to do so. So then, even though many emphasize the fact that we must spend time in true repentance in order for God to *forgive* us, it seems that we are only dealing with one side of the coin, and that side may not even actually be presented to us accurately. Ultimately, this is our *state of existence*, as *saved*, though still *imperfect* people.

While pastors are busy spending ample time preaching to their congregations that *repenting* of sin is necessary through Christ's redemption, there seems little to no time given to the subject that we are *now righteous*. I cannot help but wonder that if we were to rightly understand our true position in Christ, we might find it much easier to truly forgive because we would *know* what forgiveness is to us. A true understanding of my actual standing in Jesus would create within me a heart more tuned to Him, and much less tuned to self.

We need to learn about **all** that our salvation entails, not merely the forgiveness of sin and any need to repent. If Paul can tell me in Romans that I am justified, declared righteous, and no longer condemned, should I not become aware of all that this means to me?

If God says I am *righteous* and He tells me this in His *Word*, then this should be taught. As Chafer declares, *"So little, indeed, is the fact and value of imputed righteousness comprehended – due to a large extent to the neglect of it – that it is not easy to develop this truth to the same*

---

[19] Lewis Sperry Chafer *Systematic Theology Vol 3* (Kregel Publications, 1948, 1976), 219

level of realization to which the more accentuated verity of forgiveness of sin has attained."[20]

While God has *forgiven* us and we are taught this truth, we need to learn more about our *standing* or *position* in Christ. By not doing so, we remain in the dark concerning all that Jesus is doing in us and the benefits that are ours, in order to be more effective in accomplishing His will both in and through us. Satan likes it when we are in the dark. That is his preferred position for us, but not God's.

---

[20] Lewis Sperry Chafer *Systematic Theology Vol 3* (Kregel Publications, 1948, 1976), 219

Chapter 8

Our Sin Nature

There seems to be two extremes within the visible church today. Either people completely downplay the fact that sin exists (keeping us from God), or the opposite extreme is that all we do is *sin* and because of this, we should spend our time focusing on our sinful estate. By doing so, it is declared that we are in a much better position to eradicate that sin that exists within us, thereby pleasing our Lord.

While most believers agree that all have sinned (cf. Romans 3:23), how we *became* sinners is something about which people do *not* agree. All people are sinners, and this author believes that it is due to the fact that the apostle Paul states, "*Wherefore, as by one man sin entered into the world, and death by sin; and so death passed upon all men, for that all have sinned*," (Romans 5:12). Adam sinned, he fell, and his propensity to sin passed onto all people. How could it be otherwise if all people ultimately came from Adam's loins? If you have a corrupt tree at its root, how is it possible to have good fruit grow on that tree?

We sin because we have that *propensity* built into us, which came directly from our first parents. Because of that, it became our nature to sin and from this, we get the concept of the *sin nature*. Christ's death and resurrection free us from *having* to obey temptation because we were crucified with Him, and raised with Him. This is a fact taught in Scripture (cf. Galatians 2:20; Romans 6:6)). The problem remains that though we *are* given a new nature, our old ways and habits continue to *exist within* us, side by side. The need is to develop new habits, stemming directly from our new nature, which do not give into temptation, but instead submit to God. As we do so, He works in and through us to accomplish His will and His will does not include sinning.

As believers, we *continue* to have a propensity to sin. This built in proclivity is referred to in a variety of ways:

- *The flesh*
- *The old man*
- *The Adamic nature*
- *The sin nature*
- *The sinful nature*

Just because we become believers, it does not mean that this nature is gone. While Paul clearly tells us that we have been crucified *with* Christ, and have been freed from the *law of sin and death*, nowhere does he tell us that we have died to *sin* and *death*. We have died only to the *law* of sin and death. This means that we are no longer *slaves* to sin and death. It also means that we will still - unfortunately – sin from time to time, and we *will* die, unless the Lord comes first.

The Ideal is Not Our Reality

The ideal for each Christian is to sin less and less until they sin no more. That is the *ideal*, but it is not the reality in this life. It is like the programs put in place in manufacturing plants in which an *error free* (or Zero Percent) result is what employees shoot to accomplish. This is a nice *ideal*, but it is not *reality*. Things happen, people are not perfect, and neither is the material used to create the products. Only in a *perfect* world, complete with perfect people are no mistakes made *ever*. This is *not* a perfect world, and neither are the people in it.

Regarding the problem of whether we have a sin nature, two natures, or something else, Puritan John Owens submits these statements. *"The first problem that comes up with this question is one of semantics. For example, many prefer 'sin nature,' others prefer 'sinful nature,' and still others prefer the ambiguous 'flesh.' Whatever the specific names used for the warring parties, what is relevant is that an ongoing battle rages within the Christian.*

"The second problem is the actual definition of 'nature.' How this significant word is defined determines how one sees the distinction between the 'old man' and the 'new man' and its relevant outworking in the life of the Christian. One way to view 'nature' is to understand it as a 'capacity' within a believer. Thus, the old man is interpreted as the former way of life, that of an unbeliever. In this sense, the Christian has two competing capacities within him—the old capacity to sin and the new capacity to resist sinning. The unbeliever has no such competition within; he does not have the capacity for godliness because he has only the sin nature. That's not to say he cannot do 'good works,' but his motivation for those works is always tainted by his sinfulness. In addition, he

cannot resist sinning because he doesn't have the capacity to not sin.

*"The believer, on the other hand, has the capacity for godliness because the Spirit of God lives within him or her. He still has the capacity for sin as well, but he now has the ability to resist sin and, more importantly, the **desire to resist and to live godly**. When Christ was crucified, the old man was crucified with Him, resulting in the Christian's no longer being a slave to sin (Romans 6:6). We 'have been set free from sin and have become slaves to righteousness' (Romans 6:18).*

"At the moment of conversion, the Christian receives a new nature. It is instantaneous. Sanctification, on the other hand, is the process by which God develops our new nature, enabling us to grow into more holiness through time. This is a continuous process with many victories and defeats as the new nature battles with the 'tent' in which it resides—the old man, old nature, flesh.

"In Romans 7, Paul explains the battle that rages continually in even the most spiritually mature people. He laments that he does what he doesn't want to do and, in fact, does the evil he detests. He says that is the result of 'sin living in me' (Romans 7:20). He delights in God's law according to his "inner being," but he sees another law at work in 'the members of my body, waging war against the law of my mind and making me a prisoner of the law of sin at work within my members' (v. 23). Here is the classic example of the two entities, whatever terms they may carry. The point is that the battle is real, and it is one Christians will wage throughout their lives.

"This is why believers are encouraged to put to death the deeds of the body (Romans 8:13), to put to death that which makes a Christian sin (Colossians 3:5), and to put aside other sins such as anger, wrath, malice, etc. (Colossians 3:8). All this to say that the Christian has just one true nature, but that nature needs continual renewing (Colossians

3:10). This renewing, of course, is a lifetime process for the Christian. Even though the battle for sin is constant, we are no longer under the control of sin (Romans 6:6). The believer is truly a "new creation" in Christ (2 Corinthians 5:17), and it is Christ who will ultimately "rescue [us] from this body of death. Thanks be to God—through Jesus Christ our Lord! (Romans 7:24-25)."[21] (emphasis added)

It is as Owens says; *semantics.* Sometimes, it can be incredibly difficult to explain some of the profound truths found in Scripture. We do our best, but unlike the Bible, our own words are not inspired. Whether we say we have a sin nature, a propensity to sin or something else, the reality is that these terms and phrases are based on what is taught in Scripture.

Depravity in All Areas
The concept of sin and the total depravity of man refer to the fact that all individuals born into this world are naturally inclined to sin (cf. Jeremiah 17:9). This depravity affects every area of our life. Without God's help, we would not be able to choose to follow Christ, or to receive salvation at all. He helps by opening the eyes of individuals who are not yet saved.

Realizing that some *do* argue that man is *capable* of deciding to follow God in his (man's) fallen state, this author believes that this is not the case. Paul spends the first six chapters of Romans explaining *why* people are fallen, and *what* they are unable to do. Regarding *original sin*, at its very core, this simply refers to the very first sin committed by humanity's representative, in Adam. Beyond this, it is clear from the Genesis account that Adam and Eve were fully free to decide to follow God or Satan. In essence, they had perfect, unadulterated *free will.* This is not something that people enjoy today. Even Christians do not have perfect free will without the absence of the tendency to sin, as Adam and Eve did. We suffer from the effects of

---

[21] John Owens *Overcoming Sin and Temptation* (Crossway Books & Bibles, 2006)

sin, even after we are saved. Adam and Eve, prior to opting to believe Satan over God, had nothing going against them. They were free from all corruption, death, and sin. The only thing that made the decision for them was their wrong thinking, which stemmed from receiving incorrect information from the Tempter. That wrong thinking coupled with the completely free ability to choose their own path resulted in their failure to continue to believe God.

Had Adam and Eve *continued* to believe God in the face of temptation to call Him a liar, they would have been counted righteous, which was something they *did* lack at this point. The testing of their "faith," as it were, was to determine if they were righteous or not. They failed the test and became unrighteous.

Every other person born into this world *after* Adam and Eve is born in a fallen state, which God calls *unrighteous*. There is only one way to be declared *righteous* and that is through the receiving of His salvation, made possibly only by His death and resurrection. Once we receive this salvation, we are instantly declared to be *righteous*. This *positional* righteousness is based on *nothing* that we have done, and *everything* God has done for us. God sees every authentic believer, whether they *feel it or not*, as righteous. It is a *position*, or *standing* that can never, nor will ever be taken from us. Those who refuse God's invitation, thinking that their own righteousness is good enough, are ultimately in for a very rude (and eternal) awakening.

Like Abraham who was declared righteous (cf. Genesis 15), and yet *did* sin *after* that from time to time, was never declared unrighteous by God. Though David sinned miserably by first entertaining lustful thoughts of Bathsheba, then sleeping with her (impregnating her), and finally murdering her husband Uriah (cf. 2 Samuel 11), God did not disown David, nor did He classify His as unrighteous.

Our standing in Christ sets us apart. It is difficult to appreciate because we get tired, become saddened, angry, nervous, apprehensive, and a host of other things. We live in our corrupt flesh still, and though we are joined to Christ as new creatures, it takes much more than feeling to understand that. It takes a deep awareness that we are righteous whether we feel so or not. It is our responsibility to study His Word until we begin to grasp this magnificent truth. From there, we need to continue to study so that this awareness grows.

Chapter 9

Saved From...Saved To

After we become authentic believers, things for us have changed *permanently*. While we are *justified*, declared *righteous*, *sancti-fied*, and more, these things are only the *start* of what occurs when be receive salvation. What we are going to do in this chapter is to determine exactly what takes place when a person becomes an authentic Christian.

From and To

Many to most Christians think in terms of what we have been saved *from*, which of course is eternal separation from God in the Lake of Fire. This is obviously an important aspect of salvation. While we *should* certainly be very glad about this fact, we should also learn to focus on what we have been saved *to*. It is in understanding what we have been saved *to* that we learn about our true position and *standing* in Christ. Satan wants to keep this truth from us.

It is *not* enough to breathe a sigh of relief with respect to having been saved from the eternal wrath of God. This is not unlike the child who is always on the receiving end of his parents' wrath, but *never* their praise. We must focus on the full blessings of our salvation in Christ, which certainly includes our salvation, yet it does not stop there.

As an example, can you imagine if Christians only focused on the cross from one perspective? What if the only thing about the cross that was ever taught was God's wrath? In the cross, we certainly see His wrath at work, poured out on Jesus Christ *instead* of on humanity. However, if all we did was preach, teach, and write books on that aspect of the cross, we would only see the other side, which is God's wrath. We would never see His love. The two go hand in hand, and cannot be separated from one another. Because God is holy, just, righteous, *and* love, His love is always evidenced, yet His wrath is *only* evidenced where there is sin.

The cross of Christ portrays with excellence God's *wrath* as well as His *love*. You cannot divorce one from the other with respect to the cross of Christ. Both are manifested. Both are required. Both are part of the redemptive process.

One of the reasons we find it easier to focus on our sin is because it is always part of us, present in our daily walk. In John 16:7-11, we learn that part of the Holy Spirit's job is to convict the world of sin. In seeing the world today, it is impossible to see it and not notice sinful acts. The world is filled with sin as it pervades it on every level. The work of the Holy Spirit is required to bring a person to realize that their sin keeps them separated from God because it and it alone corrupts each individual's righteousness, which God says is as filthy rags.

As pointed out in our last chapter, John 3:18 indicates that the *"failure to believe on Christ as Savior, confirms the truth, restated more than one hundred times in the New Testament, that the **one and only condition of salvation is faith in Christ as Savior**."*[22] (emphasis added)

If that is the case – and we believe it is – then why are there attempts to change the gospel by adding requirements to it? The reality seems to be that the *only* way to salvation is by *faith*, or by *believing* in Jesus Christ.

What is Repentance?

Many believe that repentance means promising to *turn from sin*, or *to stop known sinning*. They believe this promise *must occur **before*** salvation can be received from Christ. In fact, many gospel tracts include this type of verbiage. If this is the case, then the conversions referred to previously (Zacchaeus, the thief, Cornelius, etc.) could not possibly have been *authentic*, since it is clear that there was no promise to repent that came from the individual *prior* to receiving salvation. That step is plainly absent from the narratives before salvation occurred.

To repent is often meant as *"to feel such sorrow for sin or fault as to be disposed to change one's life for the better; be penitent."*[23] However, this is the *modern* meaning of the word and it is largely derived from the history of Roman Catholicism. The idea of *penitence, penance, or being penitent* in Roman Catholicism refers to the above stated definition.

The belief that we are to *feel* or *experience* deep *remorse*, or *self-reproach* before we become saved is putting things out of order. While it *can* happen, it is not a *prerequisite* for receiving salvation as our previous examples have shown.

---

[22] Lewis Sperry Chafer *Systematic Theology Vol 3* (Kregel Publications, 1948, 1976), 218
[23] http://dictionary.reference.com/browse/repent

In its simplest and most plain sense, to repent means to change one's mind about something. In the biblical sense, it means to change one's opinion about Jesus Christ. Today, there are many who simply do not believe that Jesus Christ is:

- *God the Son*
- *Was born of a virgin*
- *Lived a sinless life*
- *Was falsely accused of blaspheme*
- *Was crucified, shedding His blood for the world*
- *Died (on Thursday) and rose again on Sunday morning*
- *Ascended to the right hand of the Father*

Ultimately, it needs to be asserted that prior to His death and resurrection from the dead, people *still* received salvation from Him, though their understanding was limited to His being God, the Savior, who was also the awaited Messiah. Their view essentially included the fact that they believed in Jesus' *mission to the world,* whatever that may have entailed and however it may have been understood by them. They had gone from *not believing* He was these things to *believing* that He was these things. It was this belief in Him that provided them salvation, just as God declared Abraham righteous because he believed the promises God had told him, as previously asserted.

When believers start placing *their* ideas on top of the biblical definition of salvation or of what the conversion experience is supposed to look like, it can and often does create problems for the converted. Questions of legitimacy come to the fore. Some believers are placing *themselves* in the position of deciding what constitutes a real conversion, and then deciding based on that definition whether the conversion is actually real or not. This leads to the frequent need to recommit their lives to God repeatedly, to ensure that they are saved.

Reproach for Sin

While we should always ensure that those we evangelize understand exactly what salvation is, the Holy Spirit ultimately opens a person's eyes to that truth. We cannot do it. That is God's work. Ours is to explain and make the truth known. God allows the lost person to see and then embrace that truth.

Putting the cart before the horse is never a good thing, primarily because it does not work. The horse needs to pull the cart. He cannot push it, nor can the cart pull the horse. Common sense dictates this to us, yet when it comes to salvation, it appears as though common sense flies out the window primarily because we have moved into the realm of the supernatural. However, the fact that salvation is supernatural in nature does *not* mean that it is received or understood outside of a logical order or disposition.

People may sense a deep conviction of their sin *after* they become saved. Authentic believers *should* (and probably *will*) sense a conviction or a chastisement from the Holy Spirit when they sin as believers in order to get to them to *rebound* quickly, once again to enjoy the full blessings of their relationship with God.

Rebound

"Rebound is the recovery procedure for loss of fellowship with God. When the believer sins, fellowship with God will be lost, this includes loss of the Filling of the Holy Spirit. Rebound is accomplished by naming our sins to God. If we acknowledge our sins, He is faithful and Righteous with the result that He forgives us our sins and purifies us from all wrongdoing. (1 John 1:9) Rebound does not require confessing to a so-called priest, fellow believers or public confession of sins before a congregation. Every believer in the Church Age is a priest who represents himself before God. It is blasphemy to confess to anyone besides God, or for anyone to assume that he has the power to forgive sins. Only God can forgive sins.

"The recovery procedure does not include penance, feeling sorry, or promising God that it will never happen again, or making pledges, vows or doing some sacrificial work for God. The sins have already been paid for by the Lord Jesus Christ on the Cross. There is nothing that can be added to His finished work (John 19:30) on the Cross. Rebound is not prayer. It is a recovery procedure. Prayer will not get through unless Rebound has preceded it as necessary. Since Rebound is not prayer, there is no requirement to go through the formality of addressing it to the Father in the name of the Son. The only thing God the Father will hear is the naming of the sins - nothing else."[24]

 R. B. Thieme, Jr., relates this to basketball. He says, *"Winning a basketball game requires basketball players to shoot and rebound the ball. When the ball leaves the hand of a shooter, arches gracefully toward the basket, drops inside the rim of the hoop, and rips through the net, he scores. But when his shot misses, the ball must be rebounded. Rebounding recovers the loose ball as it caroms off the rim or backboard. Re-*

---

[24] http://jrcyouth.com/love1.htm

bounding restores the opportunity to shoot, to score, and ultimately to win."[25]

Can you imagine a basketball player losing the ball and then dropping to his knees castigating himself? While he was busy doing that, the ball will have been rebounded by someone else, possibly on the other team. We have all seen athletes who have gotten upset with themselves when they know they have not played their best. Normally, this makes them *focus* more, not on their faults, or what they did wrong, but on what to do *better*.

So it is with the Christian, we can ill afford to bemoan our failures, or destroy ourselves emotionally thinking that this will help us become mature believers. What it does is get our eyes off the game and onto ourselves. No athlete who focuses solely on himself will win anything, unless by chance. The athlete who succeeds does so because he understands that failures are a way to success and keeps focused on the goal. In the same way, when we sin, we need to refocus ourselves on God in order to grow to maturity and win the race.

---

[25] R. B. Thieme, Jr. *Rebound & Keep Moving!* (Houston; 1972, 1993), 1

Chapter 10
Abiding IN Christ

F or the longest time, I simply did not understand what it meant to *abide* in Christ. After I became a Christian at the age of 13, I read books by A. W. Tozer and Andrew Murray. The former was easier to grasp than the latter, but that fact did not minimize the truth in both writers.

The phrase, *abide in Christ* (or the equivalents, *remain in Christ,* or *in Christ*), is one of those phrases that is difficult to connect with because in its broadest sense, it refers to the *spiritual* realm. Yet, some use it to prove that Christians can *lose* their salvation as well. Since we are *commanded* to abide, then to these individuals it makes sense that by *not* abiding, we have gone beyond the sphere of His love; therefore, they believe salvation has been lost.

To this author, that premise makes little sense biblically. We cannot remove ourselves from the Body of Christ, once we have salvation. Abiding in Christ, while a command, cannot be related to whether a person has salvation or not. Since these commands are given to *believers* (either by Christ, or one of the writers of the New Testament), it seems clear that they are given *only* to those who are already *in Christ* (by way of having received salvation), and only those who are in Christ are truly saved. Christ's command to always be *in Him*, must then refer to something else, and I believe it is best explained and summed up in the example of a parent-child relationship.

Truly, once we become part of the Body of Christ, we become **united** with the True Vine; Jesus Christ (cf. John 15:1). This vine *"is intended to be in contrast to the Israelitish vine. That vine was fruitless; but the True Vine must be fruitful and it will be. The Lord Himself will achieve this; but, from the human side, fruitfulness depends upon abiding in Christ – a relationship which the believers as branches are appointed to maintain."*[26]

On the one hand then, Christ – as the True Vine – *will* be fruitful. Yet on the other hand, *our own individual fruitfulness* depends on our daily relationship with and to Jesus Christ. The difference as described by Chafer is that of *union* vs. *communion*.[27]

Our *union* with Christ rests solely upon His shoulders. It is His responsibility. Our responsibility is in the area of *communion*. *"Abiding in Christ means unbroken fellowship with Christ."*[28] This of course, involves obeying Him; keeping His commandments. How does the Christian come to know the Lord's commandments? By reading His

---

[26] Lewis Sperry Chafer *Systematic Theology Vol 4* (Kregel Publications, 1948, 1976), 62
[27] Ibid, 62
[28] Ibid, 62

Hidden in Christ

*"If ye then be risen with Christ, seek those things which are above, where Christ sitteth on the right hand of God. **Set your affection on things above**, not on things on the earth. For ye are dead, and **your life is hid with Christ in God**,"* (Colossians 3:1-3; emphasis added)

*Even when we were dead in sins, hath quickened us together with Christ, (by grace ye are saved:) And hath raised us up together, and **made us sit together in heavenly places in Christ Jesus**,"* (Ephesians 2:5-6; emphasis added)

Every authentic Christian is NOW hidden in Christ

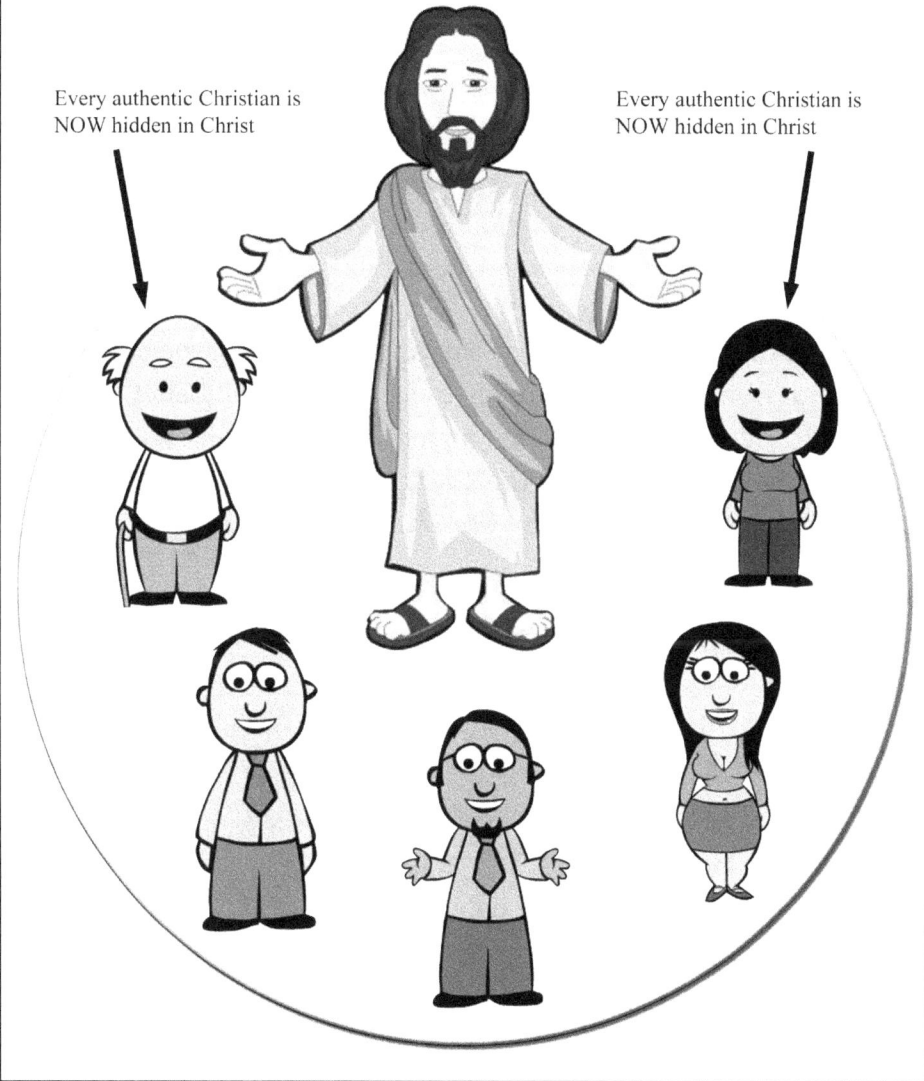

Every authentic Christian is NOW hidden in Christ

Word. As we read His Word, we get to know *how* He wants us to live and what the manner of our walk should be as we journey to the end of our lives here on the earth.

Bearing Fruit

John 15 explains this to us, from Jesus Himself. In verse 4, Jesus states, "***Abide in me***, *and I in you. As the branch cannot bear fruit of itself, except it abide in the vine; no more can ye, except ye abide in me,*" (emphasis added). Here, it is clear that *apart* from Him, we cannot bear fruit. It is that simple. This in and of itself negates the *Social Gospel*, because it is obvious that though people *can* and *do* good works, those that are not done in His strength count for nothing. The only fruit that God approves of is the fruit that flows through those who are united with Him.

Beyond this, we need to determine what Jesus is saying here. Is He saying that there is a chance that we can actually disassociate ourselves with Him, in reference to our *salvation*? I don't believe this is what He is saying at all. Paul in Romans 8 indicates that it is not possible. Toward the end of Romans 8, he explains that *nothing* that can separate us from the love of God, (cf. Romans 8:31-35). Nothing means *nothing*.

In fact, Paul explains in both Colossians and Ephesians that not only have we *died* with Christ, and have *risen* with Him, but we also currently *sit* with Him in heavenly places. Because of these facts, we are to seek the things that are above. In other words, we should focus on the fact that our citizenship is not here on the earth, but is actually in heaven with Christ.

As we begin to realize that we are *united* with Christ, *seated* with Christ, *living* with Christ, we become more aware of our actual position *in Christ*. We begin to live the Christian life much easier because of our focus. It is on Him, and not on our sin, our corruption, or what we need to do to live a life that glorifies God.

Verse 5 tells us, *"I am the vine, ye are the branches: He that abideth in me, and I in him, the same bringeth forth much fruit: for without me ye can do nothing."*

The True Vine

Jesus is the True Vine. Those who are united with Him (authentic Christians) are merely branches. Yet it is *because* we are branches that we are enabled to do things that please Him; things that are done in His power, not ours and are therefore fruitful. The branch grows and bears fruit because of its connection to the vine and root.

The individual branch has no power in and of itself to grow or produce fruit (v. 4). Remove the branch, the vine still lives. Only those branches connected to the vine, will produce fruit. That is where it needs to start. Those people who *believe* they are Christians because they *do* things in Jesus' Name may not be authentic believers. While they may thoroughly believe themselves to be authentic believers in motives and action, if they do not have genuine salvation, their works are all for nothing. True, they may have relieved pain and suffering in this world and certainly that is good from a practical and human standpoint. However, those works, *because* they were done in that individual's strength and not Jesus', have no eternal value and are therefore, *worthless*. Neither do they grow the individual toward maturity in their relationship with God.

Verse 6 of John 15 continues, *"**If a man abide not in me**, he is cast forth as a branch, and is withered; and men gather them, and cast them into the fire, and they are burned,"* (emphasis added).

We must be careful here, because it is tempting to believe that Jesus is referring to *salvation*. However, He is *not saying this* and we know this by comparing Scripture with Scripture and not resorting to *proof texting*.

What Jesus is saying is that for those who *remain in Him* or those who *continue in **communion*** with Him, good fruit will be the result. Those who do *not* continue in communion with Jesus will produce fruit that has no eternal value. Those works will be gathered and burned up in the fires of judgment. Paul echoes this truth in his first letter to the Corinthians.

*"For other foundation can no man lay than that is laid, which is Jesus Christ. Now if any man build upon this foundation gold, silver, precious stones, wood, hay, stubble; Every man's work shall be made manifest: for the day shall declare it, because it shall be revealed by fire; and the fire shall try every man's work of what sort it is. If any man's work abide which he hath built thereupon, he shall receive a reward. If any man's work shall be burned, **he shall suffer loss: but he himself shall be saved; yet so as by fire**,"* (1 Corinthians 3:11-15; emphasis added).

Here, Paul is clear that all believers' works will be subject to the judgment of Christ. This judgment does *not* determine whether a believer has salvation or not, because every authentic believer *has* salvation. Paul is warning all believers that everything we do will be judged and only those works that *abide* after being submitted to fire will receive reward. Note clearly that even on those occasions when a person's works are entirely burned up, he himself will suffer that loss, but he will *not perish*, because he has salvation.

This complements what Jesus is saying in John 15. Only those people who are in Him to begin with are authentic believers. Unbelievers *cannot* abide in Christ because they are never in *union* with Him, and therefore cannot ever be in *communion* with Him. Since they are never in *union* or *communion* with Him, they can never abide in Him. They would first have to be *in Him* in order to be able to abide in Him.

In John 15:7, Jesus further explains that, "*If ye abide in me, and my words abide in you, ye shall ask what ye will, and it shall be done unto you.*"

Asking According to His Will

Notice He is saying that *we* are to abide in Him *and* His Words are also to abide in *us.* Then the things we ask for will be accomplished. This is a problem for many because this is one of the proof texts too many use in their attempt to show that God is essentially our genie. Whatever we want, we need simply to ask and He has promised to provide!

This is *not* what Jesus is saying here. Notice that a *condition* exists. That condition is to abide or to *remain* in Him. Even though we are in Christ *positionally* through our spiritual union with Him, we must continually be in *communion* with Him so that we actively *remain* in Him (from the human side, since nothing can remove us from that position in Christ).

As we abide in Him through spiritual communion, the things we ask for *will* occur. However, we need to understand that the more we remain in communion with Jesus, the more *His* will and purposes become *our* will and purposes. Because of this, the things that we ask for are ultimately the things *He* wants to occur.

Instead of asking for a better car or a boat, or the winning numbers to the lottery, we will find ourselves praying for the lost souls of friends and family, or people at work. We will begin to realize more and more the spiritual needs of those around us and we will find ourselves desiring to be *evangelists*, fulfilling His call to the Great Commission. It is through our constant communion with Him, that we begin to see what *He* wants to achieve in and through us. Our will becomes more conformed to His and we begin to want those very same things. In this way, we continue to abide in Him.

Jesus continues with this line of thought over the next few verses in John, but also adds something. *"Herein is my Father glorified, that ye bear much fruit; so shall ye be my disciples. As the Father hath loved me, so have I loved you: continue ye in my love,"* (John 15:8-9).

Notice how He turns His attention to His Father, who is also *our* Father, because of the fact of our adoption, made possible by the Atonement? The Father is glorified when His children bear fruit. If we bear fruit, we are showing the Father that we are truly disciples of Christ. Christ then assures us that He loves us, as the Father loves Him. Because of His love, we should *continue in it*, which is another way of saying that by *abiding* in Christ, we *bear fruit*. As we *bear fruit*, we prove our love for Christ. If we *continue to bear fruit*, we are continuing in His love.

In John 15:10-12 Jesus says, *"If ye keep my commandments, ye shall abide in my love; even as I have kept my Father's commandments, and abide in his love. These things have I spoken unto you, that my joy might remain in you, and that your **joy** might be full. This is my commandment, That ye love one another, as I have loved you."* (emphasis added)

His Life <u>In</u> and <u>**Through**</u> Us

Galatians 2:20 states, *"I am crucified with Christ: nevertheless I live; yet not I, but Christ liveth in me: and the life which I now live in the flesh I live by the faith of the Son of God, who loved me, and gave himself for me."*

Paul's life was simply a vehicle for Christ to live in and through him. How does this happen? It only happens when we are in *communion* with Him. It cannot happen when we stop "abiding" in Christ, by becoming preoccupied with this world, its cares and concerns, or even its triumphs. We are not of this world, but we *are* in it (cf. John 15:19).

The Life We Now Live

Galatians 2:20

Being *in* this world causes a major distraction for the authentic Christian. Because we live in *physical* bodies, we relate to this physical world through our bodies. We see things, we smell things, we touch things, we hear things and we taste things. We become overwhelmingly conscious of these things than anything in the spiritual world.

This requires a *retraining* of our senses, so that the reality of this world diminishes in order that the spiritual will become more real. While we must retrain ourselves to do this, the rewards, according to both Paul and Jesus are great.

Since we are used to being in a world in which we relate to it physically, it does take some time to become accustomed to changing our view. A person who is born with two good eyes, but then through an accident or illness, winds up losing their sight, all is not lost, though it will certainly feel like that at the time.

Both of my eyes work fine. However, you can get a sense of what I am talking about if your eyes work as mine do by trying this experiment (which I have done). I would strongly suggest you *only* do this in your home!

The Experiment
At home, cover your eyes with a blindfold. Wear it for short periods and increase the time you wear the blindfold each day. Do this for about two weeks or more if you like. After a week or so, you should begin to notice a number of things that have changed:

- *Hearing*
- *Feeling*
- *Confidence*
- *Smell*

As you become accustomed to being "blind," you will notice that you hear things that you did not hear before. Actually, you *did* hear them previously, yet you did not really *notice* them. Now, you are noticing

110

them. Your other remaining senses will also pick up slack where your eyes no longer can.

If you stop and consider it, we *rely* heavily on our eyes. In fact, we rely much more on our eyes than any other sense we have, so it is natural that when we can no longer rely on our eyesight, we learn to rely much more on our other senses.

This is exactly what *abiding* in Christ is all about. We need to stop relying on our physical senses so much, and begin to tune into our *spiritual* senses. So how do we do this? Paul gives us the answer in Colossians 3 and Ephesians 2. Since our new creation is already seated with Christ in the heavenlies, we are to place our focus *there*, not *here*. We must learn to redirect our thoughts so that those thoughts are on heavenly things, not earthly. We have all heard the old adage, that we can be so heavenly minded that we are no earthly good. Seems unlikely, unless all a person did was sit around thinking

Blindness and the Senses

A person who is born with sight, but loses it at some point in their life, learns to adapt by using their four remaining senses. These senses become much more acute and over time, the blind person looks as though he or she is not blind when they are in surroundings with which they are completely used to being.

about heaven, and did nothing else. We *need* to practice focusing on heavenly things.

I picture myself *resting* in Christ. I see myself as already being in the heavenly realm, my life completely *hidden* in Christ (since Paul tells me this is so). When I remember to think of this, I find that my life here takes on new meaning. It automatically becomes less stressful, the temptations become less, and I find that I automatically *pray* more, *praise* more, and turn over to Him the situations that occur in my life.

It is when I turn my attention to my past *sin*, my *failures*, my *downfalls*, and then see in Scripture what my Christian life is supposed to look like, I become discouraged. I start to think that I will never "arrive," where Christ wants me to be.

The truth of the matter is that I am *already there* where He wants me to be! My life is *hidden* in Christ *now*! This is my *position in Christ*, and in order for that to become my daily experience, I need to concentrate on the fact that I am *in Him*. It is true, so I need to become more and more aware of that truth on a daily basis.

Hebrews 12:1-2 tells us "*Wherefore seeing we also are compassed about with so great a cloud of witnesses, let us lay aside every weight, and the sin which doth so easily beset us, and let us run with patience the race that is set before us, Looking unto Jesus the author and finisher of our faith; who for the joy that was set before him endured the cross, despising the shame, and is set down at the right hand of the throne of God.*"

How is it possible to "*lay aside every weight and the sin which doth so easily beset us*"? The writer of Hebrews provides the answer in the second verse where he states, "*Looking unto Jesus the author and finisher of our faith.*" This is the only way it is accomplished in our daily experience of living the Christian life. As we focus on Christ, we actually wind up laying aside (or moving away *from*) everything (including sin) that hinders us from continued communion with Christ.

Running to Lose

Show me a professional runner who looks at the ground just in front of his feet, or continually turns around to look back at other runners and I will show you a runner who not only loses the race, but also likely comes in *last* place. A good runner has his eye *way ahead of him,* down the track, toward the *finish* line. As soon as the finish line comes into view, this becomes his point of focus. He runs as if the finish line actually "pulls" him towards it.

This is what we need to do. We need to turn our attention on Jesus Christ. We need to focus on *Him*. Once we learn to turn our concentration on Him, we will find that the strength to live this life actually comes *from* Him. We will realize that as we sit there in Christ's bosom (so to speak), just as Lazarus in Abraham's bosom was content to rest on Abraham, or just as John is found to have consistently and contentedly rested his head on Jesus' chest, we will be doing the exact same thing, *spiritually*. It will become more and more alive to us over time and when problems, trials, or even persecutions come, we will already be "looking" to Jesus. We will remind ourselves that we are *in Him*, and that He lives His life in and through us.

If I am driving down the road and I happen to see a billboard with a scantily clad woman on it, I immediately have two choices. I can continue to stare at it, or I can look away. Even if I look away though, I can continue to think of that image. I must actually *replace* that image with something else.

If I am walking in the mall and in looking ahead of me see a woman dressed in tight clothing, or one with ample cleavage showing, I immediately look away and replace the image in my brain with images of my *wife*. I believe this is exactly what Paul means when he says that we are to take captive every thought (cf. 2 Corinthians 2:5).

Young men, you cannot replace these images with images of your girlfriend or even your fiancée because it could create the same result as the billboard, leading you to lust in your heart. You must replace the images with anything else that is *moral*. Baseball, fishing, words to a song, a Bible verse, or whatever you can think of that will literally move that other image out of your brain is needed (but a Bible verse is the *best option*). If you allow yourself to focus on the image on the billboard, or the physical aspects of the women at the mall, you will be *lusting* before you know it. Then, you will have to confess it before you can once again, *abide*.

We need to catch it *before* it turns to lust. We cannot control what we see in this life. We can only control *how long* we look and where it leads us. Christ within us gives us the ability to turn away, to think on those things that please Him and glorify God. As this becomes habitual, we will find ourselves lusting *less*, maturing *more*, and glorifying God in the process.

We will never perfect this in this life. When I concentrate on the fact that I am now *in Christ*, things in this life take on a different perspective. I find that I worry far less, I become agitated far less while driving on a busy road with other drivers who drive selfishly, and I find that I am filled with joy more. Why? Because it is Christ living in me, not *me* living in me and that completely changes my outlook.

You are Not Abiding When...
Those times when I am not thinking of the fact that I am *in Christ*, I wind up *not* abiding in Him. This does *not* mean I lose my salvation. It means I take over the wheel of my life and put myself in the driver's seat. I am then in control and that is when things start to go wrong. I start to believe that I can handle it, I can think my way through it, or I can discover the solution.

Jesus wants to live *His* life *in* and *through* us and He wants us to cease from working, by entering into the rest that He has provided for us.

The only way this is accomplished is by immediately giving up our *will*, our *attempts*, and our *life*, every step of the way. This is exactly what Jesus did every moment of every day as He lived on this planet. He only did what He *saw* the Father doing (cf. John 5:19). How did He *see* the Father? By faith. By seeing Himself *in the Father*. As He did this, the Father lived His life through His Son, *revealing* His will to His Son in the process. The life Jesus lived, was lived by faith in the Father. This is exactly how we are to live, by faith in God the Son.

The Circle

Notice the circle that Jesus has created here (and we have charted it out for you on the next page for all you visual learners). All that Jesus is telling us connects and continues like an unbroken circle. He is saying that by keeping His commandments, we will *remain* in His love. As we remain in His love, we will want to obey His commands.

One last section in John 15 is this, "*Greater love hath no man than this, that a man lay down his life for his friends. Ye are my friends, if ye do whatsoever I command you. Henceforth I call you not servants; for the servant knoweth not what his lord doeth: but I have called you friends; for all things that I have heard of my Father I have made known unto you,*" (John 15:13-15).

Jesus said this to His disciples not too long prior to His actual death. Who can argue with this? A person who is willing to give up his life for another is clearly showing his love for that individual. Please note that Jesus is emphasizing the fact that He gave up His life for His *friends*, and then He explains why they are His friends.

The condition set forth by Jesus to *be* His friend, requires us to do whatever it is He commands us to do, and not shrink from it. If we truly love Christ, if we desire to be His friend, then we will *obey* Him. That may sound strange, that in order to be His friend, we must obey Him, yet this is what makes us *HIS* friend!

John 15 – Abiding in Christ

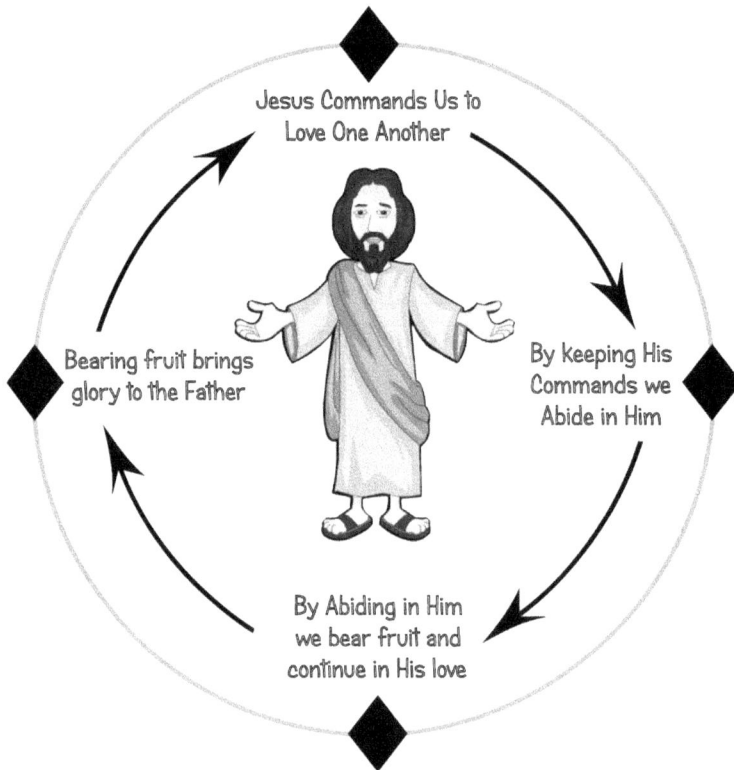

Jesus Commands Us to
Love One Another

By keeping His
Commands we
Abide in Him

Bearing fruit brings
glory to the Father

By Abiding in Him
we bear fruit and
continue in His love

Abiding in Christ is very much like a two-sided coin. All authentic believers abide in Christ in the sense that we are in UNION with Him. This is one side of the coin, which emphasizes **God's** responsibility toward authentic believers. This is our standing and it is something that will never change. The other side of the coin is **human** responsibility. We must endeavor to abide in Him through COMMUNION with Him. This is accomplished through prayer, the reading of His Word and the continued submission of ourselves to Him so that His will and purposes will be worked out in and through us, in HIS STRENGTH.

This is how we **remain** in Him, and doing so bears good fruit, fruit that is eternal, and fruit that glorifies the Father. Just as Jesus Christ needed to submit Himself to the Father each step of the way during His earthly life and ministry, so authentic believers need to do the same. Giving up our will and desires for the Father's is the only way to remain in COMMUNION with Him, the only way to BEAR FRUIT, and the only way to GLORIFY the Father. There is no other way to abide in Christ. All works done apart from our abiding in Him will burn up as they have no eternal value.

Eleazar: Servant and Friend of Abraham

Just as Eleazar was Abraham's servant, he was most assuredly his *friend* as well. How was it that he was Abraham's friend? Jesus explains a broader meaning to being His friend. The reason we are friends and not merely servants is because He takes the time to reveal to us what the Father has revealed to Him. In other words, He is taking us into his *confidence*.

As Abraham fully explained why he wanted Eleazar to go to Abraham's original land to find a wife for Isaac, so does Jesus fully explain the things we need to know in order to accomplish the tasks He gives us to do.

A Sergeant in the military simply *gives* orders. He does not take the time to explain the whys and wherefores of his orders. Those under him simply *commit to do* those orders as given. If not, they will face disciplinary action.

Jesus explains all the details that we need to know and more in order to finish the assignments He gives us. He provides information that is necessary for our *understanding*. This allows us to do a better job because we see the *goal*. The military commander does not take time to point out the goals to his subordinates. He simply gives commands. Whether they understand the reasons behind the commands or not is beside the point. Their job is to complete the tasks, *without* complaining. We are to do the same.

A Loving Parent

All authentically loving parents *do* love their children. This means that the parents want the best for the child, and is willing to do what is necessary to *help* the child achieve it.

The loving parent loves in order to get *nothing* in return. Their reward so to speak, is to see their child become an adult who is loving, caring, well-balanced, bright, articulate, self-guided and mature.

That is the payback, which in turn is instilled in any children that the child (who has now become an adult) has when they become married themselves.

Good parenting is difficult at best simply because we must get to know each of our children. While getting to know them from birth, we must also teach them about God, the need for His redemption, and their need to receive the salvation that is offered by and through Him.

In every way, parents have a difficult road to hoe. We must always seek to find the balance between chastisement and abuse, extending love vs. spoiling. Our children are not stupid. They will readily grasp when they are being browbeaten, verbally or mentally abused, or whether they are always treated with disdain. A parent's love must consistently find a way to present a balanced rearing.

The child, having been raised firmly, yet lovingly, will come to appreciate, love, and respect his parents. He will understand that though some parental dealings in his life were unpleasant, it was all for the greater good. All of it occurred in order to raise a child that grew into his own. It takes time, patience, and a great deal of love to be a good parent. Loving a child does *not* mean never taking them to task. That is called spoiling. Loving the child means praising whenever possible, chastising whenever necessary, and all under the banner of love.

In many ways, our relationship with God is like this, though of course, everything from Him to us is perfect. What makes the relationship *imperfect* is *us*. It is God's love, which creates the relationship in the first place, and it is that same love, which continues it, bringing it to its foreordained conclusion.

Our Sin is Gone
God does not spend time as our parent *continually* reminding us of

our past sin. He does not spend endless hours and days castigating us, nor does He work to constantly remind us that we are

- *Not perfect*
- *Not free of sin*
- *Not good enough*
- *Unclean*
- *Enemies*
- *Worthy of death*

Instead, God deals with us in a much more altruistic way, reminding us that we are

- *Loved*
- *Righteous*
- *Justified*
- *Sanctified and being sanctified*
- *Perfect in Christ*
- *Recipients of eternal life*
- *Adopted*
- *Friends of God*

I submit that because God's desire is to remind us that we are all of the immediate list above (and more), the list prior to that takes care of itself. In other words, as we *draw* close to God, He reveals more and more of how He views us *in Christ*. As we begin to come to terms with this truth, and see the second bulleted list become the greater reflection of reality in our lives, we automatically begin to increasingly move away from the other side of the coin; our sin and shortcomings.

When we are told to *abide in Christ*, since it cannot refer to salvation, it must refer to our *standing* vs. our *experience* (or state). Since Paul takes great pains to explain our standing in Christ (cf. Romans 8; no condemnation, and no separation), it behooves us to find out what that means because it is *there* that God wants us to live. God wants our daily experience to match our standing.

To be a friend of Jesus means that we become like Abraham's Eleazar, Abraham's most important servant, who it is said *"ruled over all that [Abraham] had,"* (Genesis 24:2). He was a man whom Abraham not only came to trust, but also loved as a son. Yet, Eleazar was a servant *still*. He did Abraham's bidding and oversaw all of Abraham's business affairs.

Because of this relationship, when Abraham's wife Sarah died, Abraham was concerned that their son Isaac did not have a spouse. Because of this, he sent Eleazar on a journey to Abraham's original country to find a suitable wife for Isaac.

Eleazar is to Abraham...

Eleazar did exactly what Abraham commanded him to do because he *loved* Abraham though he was a servant. His loyalty to Abraham was real and he likely considered Abraham his friend, though he would always be careful not to become too familiar toward Abraham by taking that relationship for granted. We see a great tenderness from Eleazar toward Abraham as shown in Genesis 24. It is obvious that Eleazar loved Abraham and it is obvious that he worshiped the same God as Abraham (cf. Genesis 24:12-14). He prayed that God would be kind to Abraham. You do not pray like this unless you care deeply for someone.

Eleazar wanted to meet Abraham's directive; his wish. If he was unable to fulfill his master's wish after attempting to do everything in his power to make it happen, then he knew that he would be released from the promise he made to Abraham (cf. Genesis 24:8). Because of this, he knew that he was not under pressure to make something happen that might not happen. Because of his great love for Abraham, that he *wanted* to fulfill the oath he had sworn. In the same way, we want to fulfill our desire to please God.

This is, in essence, our role where Jesus is concerned. Too many of us Christians spend our time trying to get God to do what *we* want Him to do *for us*. We pray for this thing, or that thing, but how often do we pray for God's will to be done? How often do we confess to God that though we *might* want something to be done our way, we ultimately only want His will in every matter we bring before Him?

This is the way it *should* be for the Christian. It is certainly no crime to bring our wants to God. To insist that He fulfill them because we are heirs of salvation is to miss the point entirely about God being God and the nature of our relationship to Him.

Eleazar had responsibilities to Abraham. As his servant, Eleazar was supposed to spend his time doing things for Abraham. He was his servant after all. At the same time, the relationship between Abraham and Eleazar had obviously gotten to a point of mutual admiration, which was based on the way Eleazar *responded* in obedience to Abraham over the years. It was this type of obedience and willingness to accomplish any task set before him by Abraham, that caused the relationship to grow to the point to which it grew.

In this way, it could be accurately stated that Eleazar *remained* in Abraham's love and trust. Why? Because of his consistent obedience to Abraham, his master. His loyalty to his master commended itself to Abraham, and because of this, Abraham gave him greater and greater responsibility until he was finally the overseer of all his business. Eleazar had become someone Abraham could trust implicitly to do what it was that he wanted done. Eleazar came to know how his master Abraham thought and how he would make his decisions relative to each situation that came up. This takes time to develop and it did develop in Eleazar.

If Eleazar were the type of servant who was half-hearted about his duties and cared little about learning the ins and outs of his responsibilities, his work would have suffered greatly. Because of this, it is extremely doubtful that Abraham would have trusted him, nor would he have given him additional responsibilities. Ultimately, is it highly unlikely that Eleazar would have been given all the responsibilities he is described as having in Genesis 24. In fact, it would have been ludicrous for Abraham to extend that amount of responsibility to Eleazar if he had not proven himself loyal and trustworthy. More than that though, Eleazar was obviously someone who could think *for* his master because of how well he had come to know him.

A Parent's Worry

Recently, my son was a bit depressed, frustrated, and tense. It was weird, though he is often straight-faced, meaning he is in that stage where he does not say a lot unless he wants to. His responses to questions are sometimes a nod of the head or a one-word reply. I know that he is not being disrespectful, just apparently conserving his energy.

At any rate, I asked him if everything was all right. He hesitated, which I immediately took to mean that not everything was all right. I pressed further and he said, "*You're not going to like what I did.*" That got me on edge, but I was also grateful he was willing to confess to something. I could see his agony as he searched for the words to say. Of course, while I waited, the worst things in the world went through my head. He finally got it out and while it was not pleasant, there are far worse things he could have done and confessed to. I was angry with him, but I was also praying...*earnestly.* I did not want to treat him with disdain, nor did I want him to think that I was so angry with him that he was no longer my son. The situation was not as bad as it could have been and after asking a few pointed questions, he was able to provide a picture of what had occurred.

As I sat there wondering how to respond to him, I realized that I needed to approach this as Christ would approach it. As I looked at my son, I could see his *pain.* He knew that what he had done was wrong and he was obviously bothered by the fact that he had done what he had done. It was clear to me that he was struggling with tears and if I did not deal with this properly, I would be helping him go down the wrong road, to *self-condemnation*. He needed to know that I considered what he had done *wrong*, but he also needed to understand that he was still part of this family. He was not being disowned. I did not hit him and I did not yell at him either.

He knew I was not happy with him. I presented my opinion firmly and with a slight increase in volume. I cited Scripture and told him how God viewed his actions. I told him directly that what he had done was unacceptable and I was glad that he saw it that way as well.

I also pointed him to several situations in the Bible that dealt with the specifics of his situation and informed him that he needed to read them, and spend time with God in prayer. Interestingly enough, when I left his room, he knew without doubt that I was *not* happy with his actions, but he also knew I still loved him a great deal. I am grateful.

Over the next day or so, I began to see my son reading his Bible more, and I noticed a change in his overall attitude. Now, had I gone in and berated him, all I would have been doing is what he was *already* doing to himself. He was fully aware that what he had done was wrong. He did not need to be reminded. He needed it confirmed to him that life would go on, that he was still loved, and that I accepted him for who he was, just as God accepted me for who I am.

We tend to believe that God *loves* (or needs) to see His children in emotional agony, because that is what somehow makes our confession *real*. Without the emotional display stemming from inward emotional upheaval, we are inclined to think there is no forgiveness.

Is this what we believe about God? Do we honestly believe that God resorts to emotional *blackmail* in order to get us to do what he wants us to do?

Remaining <u>IN</u> Jesus All the Time

©2010 F. DERUVO

WHAT?! OF ALL THE...#?@@#! I CANNOT BELIEVE THIS! (SIGH) FINE. WONDERFUL. WHAT ELSE CAN GO WRONG TODAY?

Mr. Christian is NOT abiding here, therefore he is NOT producing good fruit, that will last forever. He is NOT glorifying God.

OH MAN. THANKS FOR THE REMINDER, LORD, TO BE MORE DILIGENT! THANKS ALSO THAT MY CAR WAS NOT TOWED!

Mr. Christian IS abiding here, therefore he IS producing good fruit, that will last forever, and fruit that glorifies God.

Living for Christ

If authentic Christians lived as Christ lived, we would have far fewer problems. We would also consider *ourselves* far less. In short, we would be spending time concerned with fulfilling Jesus' will for our lives, as Jesus spent His entire life concerned with fulfilling the Father's will for His life.

D. A. Carson speaks of the fact that Jesus was not only perfect in *union* with the Father, but also perfect in *communion.*[29] This perfect communion created the constant desire in Christ to be perfectly obedient to every aspect of the Father's will. This led to perfect harmony with the Father. This is the goal of every genuine Christian. Our increasing obedience to Christ causes our communion with Christ to become more consistent in our daily experience, allowing us to actively *remain in Christ* for longer periods of time each day.

Placed in Christ

We are placed *in* Christ by the *Holy Spirit*, when we become authentic believers. This baptism into Christ's Body occurs the moment we receive salvation. Positionally, we are *in Christ*. There is nothing on the human end of things that we can do which brings this about, *except* receiving salvation. Certainly, we are unable to do what only the Holy Spirit can accomplish. At the same time, we are told in numerous instances in Scripture that it is our obligation to *remain* or *abide* in

Christ. We are essentially commanded to live our physical lives in such a way that we remain in the center of His will, just as our new creation is always in the center of His will and never sins.

Abiding in Christ is *not* something that can be accomplished with shear *willpower*. In fact, if we look carefully at one particular event in the life of Christ, we will understand that this was the *normal* way in

---

[29] D. A. Carson *The Difficult Doctrine of the Love of God*

which He approached life in general, and all the components of daily living specifically.

Chapter 11

Agony of Victory

When we consider the Garden of Gethsemane, we gain insight into *how* Jesus approached the circumstances of life. Whether each event or incidence caused such a level of stress as this one is something we do not know, but the basic way in which Christ dealt with life's trials, tribulations and struggles, is here set before us. We would do well to observe it and gain from it.

As we picture the Garden of Gethsemane and the struggle that Christ endured, we see a Man who literally *fought* with the temptation to bypass an aspect of the cross, and the desire to completely submit to

His Father's will as He had done all of His earthly life. The struggle was massive and it is very likely that Satan brought everything he had to bear on the situation, so intent was He to get Jesus to sin. Note that in the narrative, Christ's prayer was "*not my will, but thine be done.*"

Please note here that Jesus was saying that He *wanted* something else done, rather than what He knew was ahead of Him. He wanted the upcoming "cup" (whatever it was; possibly God's wrath, which was to be poured out on Him as He hung on the cross), removed from the equation (cf. Luke 22:42). It was obviously *not* a sin to *want* and/or *request* that this cup be removed. The sin would have been on *insisting* that it be removed, leaving the Father no option, in spite of the fact that God the Father had different plans. If Jesus had said something like, "Father remove this cup, or I will not go to the cross," *that* would have been sin. For Jesus to simply *request* that the cup be removed with the proviso that if *not* possible (or in God's plan), then the Father should act according to His preordained plan, was not sinful.

We face these types of decisions all the time. When we do, how often do we *demand* something of God, *without* giving Him "permission" to do whatever it is He wants to do? If all we do is come to the Father with our demands, we are *not* abiding in Him. We are abiding in ourselves. We have not learned that abiding in Christ means to *place Him and His will/desires first*

In the Garden of Gethsemane, Satan knew he was running out of time because soon, Jesus would be *dead*. Once dead, there would be no chance of Him ever sinning. In these final hours before crucifixion, Satan attempted one of several last ditch efforts to cause Christ to stumble through sin. Certainly, Christ was tempted throughout His life and His ordeal leading up the cross (and even on it), yet it is very likely that this struggle in the Garden of Gethsemane was the most *intense*.

The inner struggle, which swept over Jesus, was of such intensity that He literally sweated drops of blood (cf. Luke 23). While it is realized that people argue or debate this issue, it is generally observed that this is a literal medical phenomenon brought on by extreme stress, called *hematidrosis*. Some individuals point to the root of words of the text in an attempt to prove that Christ did *not* really sweat blood, but actually just perspired sweat itself is off the point.

Luke was a physician and he is the only one who describes the stress level in the Garden of Gethsemane from a medical perspective. As a doctor, he would have understood that what Christ experienced was a medical phenomenon. This should not surprise us due to the extreme conditions under which Christ suffered here.

This inner tension of wanting to avoid the "cup," while at the same time *only* wanting the Father's will created such an intense inner struggle, that Jesus' capillaries in His forehead literally leaked blood. Apparently, there have been other examples of this phenomenon in newborns, or people facing their own deaths. It should not surprise us that this is an actual condition; such was the intensity of stress that Jesus experienced.

The Key – Not *Willpower*, But *Submission*

Completing God's will in our strength is something that is ultimately *valueless* to God. Paul speaks of the fact that all believers' works will be judged (cf. 1 Corinthians 3). This is not for determining *salvation*, as that is already eternally gifted to the believer. The purpose of judging the works of the believer is to determine which of those works were accomplished in *God's strength* as opposed to those done in the *believer's strength*. The things done in God's strength have eternal *value* (e.g. gold, silver, and bronze; cf. 1 Corinthians), while the things done in the believer's own strength have none (wood, hay, stubble).

Had Jesus gone off to the cross under His *own* power, it would have meant nothing. What He needed to do (and did) was to submit Himself to the Father *every* step of the way. The result was that He accomplished the Father's will in the Father's strength. This is the model for us.

Socializing the Gospel with "Self" Power

The Emergent Church today is busy emphasizing a *Social Gospel*. Many of the leaders within the Emergent Church believe and teach that by merely *doing* "good works," we become identified with Jesus and are then in *union* with Him. Some have come right out and stated that this constitutes salvation.

Essentially then, a Buddhist who spends his life doing good works is said by some leaders within the Emergent movement, to already *be a Christian*, though the Buddhist would say that they are *Buddhist*, not Christian. In effect, this *buries* Christianity within the framework of other religions, based on the good works that these individuals perform. In other words, Christianity becomes a works-based religion, instead of one that is faith-based.

It is abundantly clear from Scripture that our good works cannot save us (cf. Ephesians 2:8-10). Even after receiving salvation, works performed under our own power are worth nothing, as stated. This does not seem to matter to these individuals because they emphasize only what Jesus says in the gospels, and specifically the Beatitudes of Matthew 5-7.

Valueless works, no matter how good they appear to be *externally*, will be burned in the fire of judgment. In fact, Paul clearly speaks of those individuals who may spend their entire lives (once they become believers), doing one good work after another, but they have obviously done these works in their own strength because all their works burn up, though they themselves are saved, barely escaping the flames (cf. 1 Corinthians 3). This is important for us to note. The works we consider good are not good *unless* done in God's strength and as part of His will for us.

Believers have four choices:

1. *To do our own thing in our own strength*
2. *To do God's will in our own strength*
3. *To do what we think is God's will in our own strength*
4. *To do God's will in God's strength*

It should be clear by this point that only the last one (#4) earns *value*. It does so because it removes *self* from the picture, and it brings great glory to God. All the other options keep *self* firmly enthroned, and because of that, bring God no glory at all.

The believer who does numbers 2 or 3 may do things that *look* as though they are God's will, but in the end are *not*. This is the problem with the *Social Gospel*. It emphasizes works by the individual's own willpower and strength. As far as the world is concerned, seeing a professing Christian (or an authentic one for that matter) do good things for people *may* offer convincing proof that the individual is truly a Christian. Jesus indicates that this is *not* how it works though.

In His parable of the Sheep and the Goats (cf. Matthew 25), he points out that it is *not* those who *do things in His Name* that are the authentic believers. Those individuals who were actually in *relationship with Jesus* turn out to be true believers. His words, "*Depart from me...I never **knew** you*" are shockingly tragic because He is saying that *only* those who were in *relationship* with Him were the ones whom He *knew*. The others were merely pretenders, simply using His Name for their own self-glorification or self-aggrandizement.

Many people will find themselves in the Lake of Fire after their judgment. They will be utterly shocked to realize that this is their "reward" for their life, especially after all they accomplished *for* Christ (they believe), and in His Name. This is *heartrending* and *frighten-*

ing when seriously contemplated. To think that there will be people who spent their life on earth doing things in Jesus' Name, yet because He did not *know* them at all (did not have actual salvation), what they did, not only did not bring Him glory, but actually brought *dishonor* to Him. It is on this basis (that He did not know them), that they will be cast in the Lake of Fire.

It was not long ago when a well-known talk show host had a famous religious personality on his show. The woman he had on the show was known for the ministry she had with her husband before things went seriously downhill. The poor woman at that point was at death's door due to cancer. Well under 100 pounds, she had difficulty breathing, and looked not much better than a skeleton with skin.

During the course of their conversation, the talk show host asked her why she thought God had chosen her for her particular ministry. Her response was (paraphrased; emphasis added), *"I believe He picked me because He needed someone He could **trust**."* She also responded when asked that yes, she was a bit afraid of her upcoming death, but she believed that when she awoke (in the afterlife), she would be in the hands of Jesus. I seriously hope that this turned out to be the case.

The potential tragedy here is manifold. Here was a woman who, along with her husband (from which she later divorced because of his sexual proclivities), spent years on the television literally *panhandling* in God's Name. Together, they built up a huge empire, which they *believed* was the result of God's blessing and will for them. Yet, they ultimately went down in smoke. They literally crashed and burned because of the public improprieties of *both* of them.

Did this woman stand before Jesus and hear the words *"Well done,"* or did she hear, *"Depart from me"*? Of course, that is in the Lord's hands, but why was I so *scared* for this woman? I sensed this tremendous *fear* for her. It felt like she did not have the slightest clue about salvation. In my heart, I felt that she was not an authentic believer and all I could do was *hope* and pray that I was wrong.

I am **not** saying that I *knew* she was not a believer, or that I pronounced her an unbeliever. I am simply saying that it *seemed* she was not a believer, based on the testimony of her life and words. Only God knows the truth.

Does Christ *Know* You?

There are many alive today who have ministries for God. They do all that they do in His *Name*. They believe that they bring great glory to God, yet in many cases, their lives *look* as if they do not. They appear as if they are merely serving themselves and using God as the means through which they can fulfill their own personal dreams and desires. Why do I believe this? Because many of these individuals preach a gospel that is *not* the same gospel that Jesus, Paul, Peter, John or any of the writers of the New Testament preached.

In many cases, the people we see on the television and hear on the radio proclaim that God is there for *us*, and all we need to do is *ask* Him (no, make that, *demand* of Him, via "name it-claim it") and He will do *for us*. He is standing by for that purpose. Ask away.

A number of years ago, I recall listening to this same woman just referred to discussing Jesus and whether or not Jesus would wear $500 suits (like her husband did then). She happened to be on the same talk show with the same host. Her response, without even pausing was that she believed Jesus would be a *man of the times*, and therefore *would* wear expensive suits. The absolute temerity of that response is startling!

Had Jesus wanted to have done that, He could have *easily* been a man of His *own* time and dressed as the Pharisees dressed, with their expensive robes and clothing! Jesus did *not* dress like them *then*, and

He would certainly not dress like some of the television preachers of today!

The view that Jesus would have indulged in the financial waste of our times, or that God the Father is there to grant us personal wishes, is *reprehensible*. God is in no way, our *genie*. He does *not* exist to fulfill our dreams. He exists to have *His* will accomplished *by us* and all of His Creation. He did not create us for *our* good pleasure, but for *His*. He did not leave us here after we become authentic believers, in order to become *our servants*. He leaves us here after we become believers, in order that we might *fulfill* His *will*, in His *way*, and in His *strength*.

Unlike what too many preach, God does *not* want us physically rich. He does not necessarily want us perfectly healthy (physically), and the fact that we remain in dying bodies proves it (thanks to our own sin nature). Moreover, He does not want us focusing on getting the best *job*, the best *car*, the best-looking *spouse*, and the perfect *kids*. He does *not* want us to think that all we merely need to do is rub the lamp of His Word three times and we get all the wishes we could ever hope to have in this life.

What God *wants* is for authentic believers to submit themselves to Him in order that His purposes will be perfectly accomplished in and through us. He wants a Body of believers who have turned their backs on Self, and have learned to fix their eyes on Jesus only (cf. Hebrews 12:1-2).

Chapter 12

Fixing Our Eyes On Him

T he only way to remain *in Christ*, is to keep our eyes *fixed* on Him. We cannot be looking at our sinfulness *and* seeing Him at the same time. This is certainly not to say that the Holy Spirit will never point out our sin, but it *is* to say that we are to confess it, and move on, continuing in step with the Holy Spirit.

More than one person refers to this as *rebounding*. It is the process by which we recognize our individual sins as quickly as they are brought to our attention, and then *confess* them to the Lord, agreeing with Him that they are, indeed, sinful. We are told in 1 John 1:9, "*If we confess our sins, he is faithful and just to forgive us our sins, and to cleanse us from all unrighteousness."*

Keeping the List Short

But wasn't all of our sin – *past, present, and future – forgiven* the moment we placed our faith and trust in Christ for salvation? Absolutely, however, as we sin and as the Holy Spirit brings this to our attention, we need to stop and *confess it*. When we confess something, we are *agreeing* with God that what we did was in fact, sin. When we confess, we are not making excuses, or attempting to shift the blame to someone else. We are accepting full responsibility for our own actions, thoughts, and words.

When I say that we need to *confess* our sin, exactly what am I talking about here? Am I saying that we need to take out a whip, and whip ourselves until we bleed? Am I saying that we need to do some other form of penance in order for God to *notice* that I am serious about how bad I feel about my sin? Am I indicating that we need to wallow in sorrow and remorse, before God will realize that I am sincerely *repentant* about my sin?

NO! God does not expect us to create feelings of self-condemnation, self-denigration, remorse, or anything else. It all depends upon the sin itself, doesn't it? If someone steals something from a retail store, the level of the sin is far greater than if someone accidentally (or even intentionally) takes a pen from work that is not his or hers to take. The consequences of those sins are completely different. While it is true that sin is sin, who would argue that in this life, consequences of all sin are the same?

If I say something asinine to my wife, or respond to her in an irritated fashion, as *soon as I realize what I have done*, is the time to confess to her that I was wrong. My wife, also a Christian and a very loving woman, then has the opportunity to forgive me of my stupidity and life can move on. She does *not* expect me to *condemn* myself, or beat myself up physically or emotionally in order to *prove* to her that I am sincere.

What about if a husband cheated on his wife? The circumstances and level of sin are *different*. That husband has violated a trust, which he promised in his original marriage vows that he would never do. He fell, and he fell big time. This creates untold havoc on any marriage. If that other woman with whom the husband had an affair is married, it also involves *her spouse*. This not only becomes extremely complicated, but the consequences are ramped up accordingly.

Each case is determined by the level or intensity of sin, which is directly related to the intensity of consequences. The consequences are in direct measure to the intensity of the sin. Forgiveness is not dependent upon the intensity of the sin, and all sin no matter how big or small, needs to be confessed. Thankfully, all sin has already had forgiveness applied to it, for the Christian.

Quick to Forgive

God does not react to us as other people react to us. God, according to John, is *quick* to forgive when He sees genuine remorse leading to confession. He does not want us estranged from Him, nor does He want our fellowship with Him damaged. If we sincerely admit our sin to Him, He is *just* and faithful to forgive.

Again, depending upon the sin, we may come to Him with a good deal of sorrow. We may feel terrible about what we have done and when we kneel before Him, that emotion is evidenced to Him. That is a natural part of repenting of our sin, *if* the nature of the sin is such that it causes us to see how much we have hurt someone else.

If I take a pen from work that does not belong to me, I am not going to approach God with tears streaming down my face. I am going to approach Him feeling stupid and wondering why I did what I did and I will confess it to Him and return the pen the next day when I return to work.

Now, if I make it a habit of taking pens, pencils, paper, and other items from work because I do not want to spend my money on obtaining them legitimately, then I have a problem. The Holy Spirit will work to bring this problem to light and when I finally realize it, it may well hit me very hard. In such a case, I may be very humbled or even brought to tears because of my sin. Restitution will be part of the solution, but God's forgiveness – provided I am sincerely and humbly penitent in my attitude – is quickly forthcoming. Notice though that though God has forgiven me, consequences will often *remain*. He promises only to forgive. He does *not* promise to remove or change the consequences.

Let's say – for the sake of argument – that a Christian friend of mine went to a party, fell back into sin, got drunk and then drove home with a blood-alcohol content way over the limit. On the way home, he runs a stoplight and plows broadside into someone crossing the same intersection, in which they had the right of way. In the process, the driver on in the other car was killed. What do you think is going to happen? Will God forgive my friend? Yes, He will forgive. Will He change the consequences of my friend's actions? Probably not. He is *not* obligated to do so, nor should He.

Though God will have forgiven him, there is the likelihood that the people involved – because of the death caused by his actions – may not forgive, or may have a very difficult time forgiving. My friend will also face fines and/or prison time for his actions. Does he deserve these things? Of course! Simply because he can say that he is a Christian does not exempt him from legal consequences. Being a Christian is not his "get out of jail" card. In fact, think of the terrible testimony that comes from a Christian doing something so stupid and reckless. Not only has that Christian ruined his reputation, but also because he *says* he is a Christian, he has dragged God's Name through the mud. How does that bring anyone to Christ?

The seriousness of the sin and its effect on others often determines the level of sorrow and remorse when coming to God for forgiveness. We do not need to *work* it up, or create it within ourselves, nor do we need to artificially prove to God that we are really, *really sorry* for our sin, and hopefully He will see that because our knees are bleeding from crawling across the concrete in an attempt to prove to Him our truly penitent attitude!

God is not stupid. He *knows* when we are sincere in our confessions of sin to Him. He does not need us to prove it to Him *externally*, because He sees *the heart*. While we can fool people at times, we can never fool God.

Drumming Up Pride

All of the effort we may put into creating sorrow, remorse, self-condemnation, and the rest, keeps our eyes firmly fixed on *ourselves*. But what are we told to do in the book of Hebrews? "*Wherefore seeing we also are compassed about with so great a cloud of witnesses, let us lay aside every weight, and the sin which doth so easily beset us, and let us run with patience the race that is set before us, **Looking unto Jesus the author and finisher of our faith**; who for the joy that was set before him endured the cross, despising the shame, and is set down at the right hand of the throne of God,*" (Hebrews 12:1-2; emphasis added).

How is it possible to *look* to, or *fix* our eyes on Jesus if we are continually focusing on our sin? How can we possibly move ahead and "*lay aside every weight, and the sin which doth so easily beset us*" if all we are concerned with is our *sin*? I submit that if we create the habit of fixing our eyes on Jesus, we will sin *less*. When we *do* sin, we will confess it with sincerity and move on, in greater submission to Jesus.

To believe we need to create a level of emotional remorse within ourselves is an insidious form of *pride*. This is another way that Satan keeps our eyes on ourselves, and off Christ. By continually focusing on how *bad* we are, how *corrupt*, how *sinful*, we are actually *feeding our pride* because the attention is on ourselves. Jesus wants us to *fix* our eyes on Him. Luke 9:62 says, "*And Jesus said unto him, No man, having put his hand to the plough, and looking back, is fit for the king-dom of God.*" I realize that Jesus had just told a person who wanted to go home and say "good-bye" to everyone that if he wanted to do that, he was in effect moving ahead while looking backwards. However, the truth remains that if all we do is look back, worrying about the things that have already come and gone, we are not *truly* ready for God's kingdom.

Paul tells us, "*Not as though I had already attained, either were already perfect: but I follow after, if that I may apprehend that for which also I am apprehended of Christ Jesus. Brethren, I count not myself to have apprehended: but this one thing I do, forgetting those things which are behind, and reaching forth unto those things which are before, I press toward the mark for the prize of the high calling of God in Christ Jesus,*" (Philippians 3:12-14). Paul is here admitting that he is *not* perfect, nor has he arrived at the place where God intends all authentic believ-ers to be. He is also saying that he did not waste time focusing on things in the past; mistakes he may have made, sins he committed. These things keep us *bound* to the past (with the focus on us), and Paul says we should *press on* toward that mark. The mark is the end of the race, when we die, where Jesus awaits our arrival. We must al-ways keep that in view, because that alone creates an outlook in the believer, which *stimulates* our desire to please God by obeying Him and submitting to Him every step of the way.

The things around them or behind them do not distract a person who runs a race. They have their eyes on the goal, which is the finish line. If all they did was look behind them constantly, or become distracted by what is going on at the sidelines, they would not only *not* win the race, but there is an excellent chance they would run out of bounds, or trip and fall over something or someone.

Abiding in Christ?

The professional runner must remain focused. We have all seen races where someone fell or did not run their best. They know what they did wrong and they do not like it. However, even if they decide to break down in tears, deriding themselves for their mistake, does it help them win that race? No, that one is over. Better to get working on the next one. We learn the same thing from our sins and failures. They do not condemn us, but these experiences allow us to grow and not make the same mistakes the next time.

They use their failures to make themselves a better runner, so that next time, they will not make the same mistake.

Abiding vs. Not Abiding

As the chart called "Abiding in Christ?" on the next page shows, the top illustration highlights a person whose mind is *fixed on Jesus*. Because of this, he reacts to situations as Jesus would react. That driver is avoiding problems even before they have a chance to start. His communion with Christ keeps him from sin.

This is not the case with the driver in the *bottom* illustration. Because he has stopped "abiding" (*communing with Jesus, keeping his mind fixed and focused on Him*), he is living in his flesh. Because he is living in his flesh, he produces nothing good. There is no good fruit here because he is angry and becoming angrier. Chances are good that he will do something stupid based on his fleshly anger.

However, the driver in the top illustration has his mind fixed on Jesus. Because of this, he reacts out of his spiritual connection with Christ, not out of his flesh. The result of this continued communion with Him is that he bears good fruit. He is not angry. He does not take things personally, and he even looks for ways to *avoid* problems for himself and others. Both men have salvation, however only one is *acting as though he is saved*.

By placing and keeping our eyes fixed on Jesus, that action alone creates one of the greatest helps in avoiding sin. The more we read the Bible (His Word), the more we get to know Jesus. The more we get to know Him, the more He is on our mind. The more He is on our mind, the less chance there will be of sinning when temptation comes along. This is the goal of the Christian. This is how we align our physical walk with our spiritual standing. If we do not do this, then all that this physical life promotes serves to constantly distract us.

Chapter 13

Our Divine Riches: The Greatest Secret

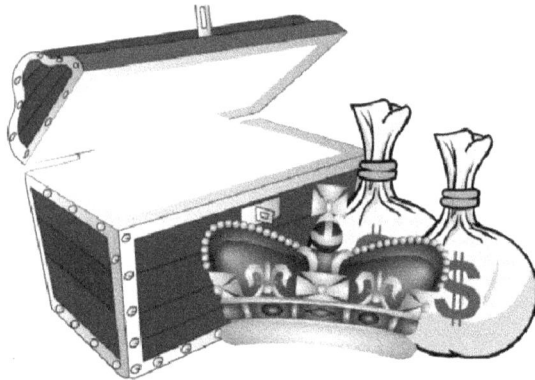

N ow that we have a clear understanding of sin, repentance, and salvation, in order to truly live the Christian life, we have to recognize our divine riches. However, what possible good can come from our riches in the heavenly realms *now*, if we are *unaware* that they do indeed exist? Our divine riches in Christ are *manifold*, and they do benefit us *now*. While we will not fully benefit from our salvation until we leave this mortal body, our soul prospers, being *in Christ*. These divine riches or blessings are ours simply because of our union with Christ. Yet, Satan would prefer that we have no knowledge of the entirety of these riches, which we already possess.

It is difficult for us to comprehend the fact that we are blessed with these blessings and that is largely because of the fact that we exist in the physical, not spiritual realm. While our spirit is seated with Christ in the heavenlies (cf. Ephesians 2), our life is largely experienced here, on the earth. We experience this life through our physical senses of touch, sight, sound, taste, and smell. These senses understood through our physical bodies, are what give life meaning for us here.

Due to our own physical limitations, attempting to understand the spiritual from *within* the physical is easier said than done. This is why God loves to see our *faith* in Him. The blessings we have are as much as we will ever have, and not something that we grow into, according to Chafer.[30]

Chafer indicates three other things in connection with these blessings. 1) We cannot earn them, as they are completely gifted to us by God, 2) they are eternal, and 3) they are known and understood only as God reveals them.[31]

Chafer outlines the 33 divine riches in his systematic theology, the third volume, pages 234 – 265. We are not going to list every individual blessing here, but we will list and discuss the obvious ones. These need to be known and understood by every believer, as this is what makes a difference in the life of the authentic Christian.

1. Eternal Plan of God
The first group of blessings or divine riches comes under the umbrel-

---

[30] Lewis Sperry Chafer *Systematic Theology Vol 4* (Kregel Publications, 1948, 1976), 233
[31] Ibid, 233-234

la of being in *God's eternal plan*. This speaks of the fact that these things were decided before the foundations of the world were laid. It was before the first human being was created.

While God obviously has the capacity to the see the beginning from the end (cf. Revelation 21:6), He plans all things. He did not merely look into the future to know what everyone would do and plan around that. He directs the affairs of men (cf. Proverbs 16:9; see also the book of Job and the life of Christ).

God *determined* prior to the start of any creative work on His part what would take place. He left nothing up to chance, even creating some to fulfill "ignoble" purposes (cf. Romans 9:14-24), so that those who were recipients of His mercy for salvation would bring glory to Him.

A. Foreknown

Chafer notes the first of five terms employed to undergird the meaning of sovereignty. This first one is foreknown and means *"that God foreknew from all eternity every step in the entire program of this universe to its minutest detail."*[32]

B. Predestinated

This word emphasizes God's work of determining before the foundations of the earth all of what will come to pass. *"In its New Testament use it refers only to that which God has predetermined for His elect."*[33] These first two terms (foreknown and predestinated) are often confusing because they seem similar. Paul says that those He foreknew, He also predestinated (cf. Romans 8:29). However, Chafer comments, *"The question of whether, in point of time, foreknowledge, precedes predestination, or predestination precedes foreknowledge, is not only useless but wholly uncalled for. God could not predestinate what*

---

[32] Lewis Sperry Chafer *Systematic Theology Vol 3* (Kregel Publications, 1948, 1976), 235

[33] Ibid, 235

He did not foreknow. Nor could He foreknow as certain to come to pass that which He had not made certain by predestination."[34]

C. Elect of God

The use of this phrase relates to the *destiny* of authentic Christians. Christians are *"the elect in the present age and will manifest the grace of God in future ages (cf. 1 Thess. 1:4; 1 Pet. 1:2; Rom. 8:33; Col. 3:12; Titus 1:1)."*[35]

D. Chosen

We are chosen by God for His purposes. No one knows the hows, whys, and wherefores of God's choosing. We know that it exists.

E. Called

Being called by God is related to His choice. He foreknew and pre-destinated some to salvation. Because of this, He elects, chooses and calls. It is this call (or effectual calling) which as Chafer states, *"inclines the heart to glad acceptance of it."*[36]

2. Redeemed

The work of God in redemption is fully God's work. He redeems the elect. It is this position by which the elect are then justified, glorified and sanctified.

3. Reconciled

Because God reconciles the believer, the wall that cut God off from humanity is taken down. As Paul tells us in Romans 8:1, those who are in Christ are no longer condemned. That is a thing of the past, forever. Reconciliation is that which takes those who were far away from God and allows them to draw close to Him. This work, done by God alone replaces condemnation with eternal peace with God.

---

[34] Lewis Sperry Chafer *Systematic Theology Vol 3* (Kregel Publications, 1948, 1976), 235

[35] Ibid, 236

[36] Ibid, 236

4. Related to God through Propitiation

Because of the death of Jesus Christ, God is able to be favorably inclined toward sinners, and especially the elect.   Because authentic believers continue to sin after salvation has been received, God is forever able to continue in relationship with the sinful believer because of this propitious nature of God the Father.

5. Forgiven All Trespasses

This harkens back to Romans 8, where Paul states clearly that we are no longer condemned. This is so because all of our sins – past, present, and future – are completely forgiven. God does not remember them any longer (cf. Colossians 2:13). This is our position or standing in Jesus. To the Father, we are just as righteous as Jesus Christ is because it is His righteousness, which has been imputed to us. His righteousness covers us and cancels out our sin.

6. Vitally Conjoined to Christ for the Judgment of the Old Man

Christ's death was a judgment on our sin nature. Because we were baptized into Christ, we were baptized into His death and then His resurrection. Because sin was judged perfectly on Christ, as He hung dying on Calvary's cross, God is free to see our sin nature as something that has already been judged.

Nothing the Christian can do will make this happen. It has *already* happened and it is the job of the Christian to *reckon* it, to *believe* it, to *accept* that it is true.

7. Free from the Law

The authentic believer is free from the mandates of the Law for salvation. The Law is unable to grant salvation. It is only able to point out error. It has no capacity to make a person clean, or righteous.

Because the authentic believer has been freed from the Law of sin and death, we are no longer obligated to follow its demands hoping to be received by God. As authentic believers, we follow the dictates of the Law *because* God already receives us.

8. Children of God
We have become children of God, which means we have been *Born again, regenerated, quickened,* and called *Sons of God* and ultimately, a *new creation*. All things are new. The old is gone forever.

9. Adopted
We cry "Abba, Father" because we have been adopted into God's family. This is an enormous benefit! God is our Father! Chafer notes that our adoption refers to, "*a divine act by which one already a child by actual birth through the Spirit of God is placed forward as an adult son in his relation to God. At the moment of regeneration, the believer, being born of God and therefore the legitimate offspring of God, is advanced in relationship and responsibility to the position of an adult son.*"[37]

10. Acceptable to God by Jesus Christ
A number of things occur within the authentic believer, which make us acceptable to God because of the work of Jesus Christ. First, we are m*ade righteous.* Christ's righteousness is imputed to us (cf. 2 Corinthians 5:21). God sees us, yet does not see any unrighteousness in us, but Christ's righteousness only.

Second, we are *sanctified positionally.* The authentic believer is instantly made perfect *in Christ.* That is our position and it is from this position that we *should* live. However, we remain in this world, with our sin nature intact, which keeps us from arriving at a sinless state of perfection in this life. Our position in Christ is different from our daily experience. We are sanctified because God sets us apart. It is because we are set apart, that we should mirror our position, in this world.

---

[37] Lewis Sperry Chafer *Systematic Theology Vol 3* (Kregel Publications, 1948, 1976), 242

Third, each authentic believer has been *perfected forever* (cf. Hebrews 10:14). This again refers to our standing in Christ. Because I am a new creation, and because I am *in Christ* positionally, and because I am seated with Him in the heavenly realms (cf. Ephesians 2), this new creation is unable to sin. Positionally, the authentic believer is perfect, yet not in this life.

Fourth, each believer is *made accepted in the beloved*. Chafer points out that the word "made" is something that signifies God's work, not ours. God makes us accepted in the beloved (cf. Ephesians 1:6). Everyone who is truly saved is fully accepted by God the Father, based on the propitiation of Jesus Christ.

11. Justified

To be justified means that God recognizes our righteousness, which is not really ours, but Christ's having been imputed to each believer. It is because God declares us righteous, that He also declares us *just*.

12. Made Nigh

The fact that we are made righteous, justified, and sanctified, brings us close to God. We are no longer strangers, far off, but sons who may draw near (cf. Ephesians 2:13).

13. Delivered from the Power of Darkness

This is such an extremely important blessing to understand. What this ultimately means is that the powers of darkness, including Satan himself have no power over us, except what God allows (cf. Colossians 1:13; 2 Corinthians 4:3-4; Ephesians 2:1-2). Essentially, because we have been delivered from them, we are freed from having to obey their desires in the form of temptation. In Christ, we can say "NO!" because we are not slaves to them, nor are we under their thumb. We are free from their power and it is up to us in Christ to say "NO!"

14. Translated into the Kingdom of the Son of His Love

What better blessing could there possibly be? Whereas once we were dead in our trespasses and sins, we have now been literally taken out of that kingdom – the kingdom of death – and lovingly planted firmly in the Kingdom of Jesus Christ! We believers need to focus in on that fact. We must meditate on it and all that it promotes within us (cf. John 3:5; Colossians 1:13).

Our current obligation is to live *as if we are in God's Kingdom* because we *are* in His Kingdom, whether we feel it or not. As citizens of this Kingdom, we must act accordingly and doing the things that bring dishonor to God is not the way to do that (cf. 1 Thessalonians 2:12; 2 Peter 1:11).

15. On the Rock, Christ Jesus

Because we are planted on the Rock of Jesus Christ, nothing will ever be able to separate us from Him or His love (Romans 8). No longer condemned, we can never be separated from Him. There is no greater position than to be firmly planted on the Rock of Christ, within the Kingdom of Christ (cf. Matthew 7:24-27; 1 Corinthians 32:9-15).

16. Heavenly Citizens

We are citizens of heaven! What a blessing and for us to begin to realize what that entails, means a complete change in our life and outlook! As citizens, nothing can touch our new creation. Though men might kill the body, our newly created spirit through the new birth is safely tucked away in Jesus (cf. Philippians 3:20; Luke 10:20; Hebrews 12:22).

17. Of the Family and Household of God

As part of God's family and household, God will do whatever is necessary to protect us from the forces of darkness. Just as Job in the Old Testament had a hedge planted around him, so are we encircled with God's protective hedge, ensuring that we are His family and that His love surrounds us. We must endeavor to live in such a way that the Name of Christ (our family Name) is never dishonored (cf. Ephesians 2:19; Galatians 6:10; 2 Timothy 2:19).

18. In the Fellowship of the Saints

Whether we realize it or not, we enjoy the fellowship of the other saints, who are members of Christ's Body. This fellowship is perfect and complete (cf. John 17:11, 21-23).

19. Having Access to God

We are told – because of our position in Christ – that we can come before the Father boldly. This does not mean with an attitude of disrespect. It means that we do not have to fear coming before Him to make our requests known.

Unlike the Old Testament High Priest who could only come before the Ark of the Covenant, which contained the Mercy Seat, once per year and then only with blood, the blood of Christ has completely cleansed our lives and in Him, we are pure. Because we are pure, we do not have to fear the Father's wrath or retribution. We are loved, and accepted by the Father, just as He loves and accepts Jesus Christ (cf. Romans 5:2; 2 Corinthians 3:18).

20. His Inheritance

What a blessing! We are literally the Father's inheritance through the Son! He will never cast us out! We are His forever! (cf. Ephesians 1:18; John 17:22; Colossians 3:4).

21. Vitally United to the Father, the Son, and the Holy Spirit

A break in union with the Father, the Son and the Holy Spirit will *never* occur. We are forever united with them and we are partakers of the divine nature, which allows us to live a holy life, fully pleasing to God, our Father in Jesus Christ, through the empowering of the Holy Spirit (cf. 1 Thessalonians 1:1; Ephesians 4:6; Romans 8:1; John 14:20; Romans 8:9; 1 Corinthians 2:12).

22. Glorified

Positionally, we are fully glorified. Our sin nature is gone (in Christ), and we await that reality for our bodies as well (cf. Romans 4:17; Romans 8:18; Colossians 3:4).

23. Complete in Him

In Christ, there is nothing that we need. We have everything that pertains to life and godliness and we are now holy and perfect in our position in Christ. One day, immediately after our death, we will be perfect in experience (cf. Colossians 2:9-10).

24. Possessing Every Spiritual Blessing

We are blessed beyond measure. We must take the time to meditate on this truth. We must ask God to enlighten us to the full measure of insight regarding these wonderful blessings. They are there for us, in order that we might glorify Him, bringing only honor to His Name (cf. Ephesians 1:3).

• Both Sides of the Cross

As noted, we have *not listed all 33* of the divine riches we, as authentic believers have in Christ. Search the Scriptures to find the other nine. It is important for the Christian to understand *both* sides of the cross; both God's wrath and His love. It was His love that prompted God the Son to take on the likeness of sinful flesh (cf. Romans 8:3; Philippians 2:7). This act of death on a cross, allowed God to pour His wrath onto His Son. That wrath, since it was poured out on Christ, will never need to be poured out on those who call on the Name of Jesus for salvation.

Christians need to spend time learning, understanding, and knowing the tremendous riches we have in Christ. While we *must* know what Jesus accomplished for us, with respect to God's wrath, we must not stop there, focusing only on how much God hates sin. We must continue on, unlocking the reality and full measure of God's grace and love seen not only in His wrath poured out on Jesus, but the riches freely given to those He calls His own.

Focusing on only one aspect of the cross (whether His wrath of His riches), creates Christians who are unbalanced and immature. It is in knowing that Jesus not only paid the debt we created through our sin, but also bestowed on us greater riches than could ever possibly be understood in this life, that we begin to more naturally move away from sin, and toward Jesus – living the Christian life in joy.

Chapter 14

Pursuing Holiness?

The emphasis for Christians to move toward holiness within certain circles of Christendom has some merit. However, I cannot help but wonder whether the process by which we become holy in our daily lives is being emphasized in a way that puts too much focus on *us*.

Jesus really gave us two positives, which He said sum up the entire law:

1. *That we should love God with all our heart, soul, and mind,* and
2. *We should love our neighbor as ourselves*

That is What We Are to Do!

In those two commands, the emphasis is on what we *should be doing*. Often, when pursuing holiness, the emphasis is on what we should *not* be doing. Is it easier to reach out in love toward people, or is it easier to focus on **me**? You will notice that in both of the commands above, the emphasis by Jesus is *away from yourself*. It is by *not* considering your own needs, *not* focusing on yourself that frees us to focus on the needs of others.

There are some wonderful books out there and one in particular is by Jerry Bridges titled, *The Pursuit of Holiness*. I believe Bridges makes some very cogent and worthwhile points. I also believe that some of the points he makes may create a tendency to focus on ourselves, resulting in frustration and a sense that we are never doing things well enough, which draws us further into a focus on self.

A Commitment to a Life of Holiness

In referencing our propensity to sin he states, "*We must recognize that we have developed habit patterns of sin. We have developed the habit of shading the facts a little bit when it is to our advantage. We have developed the habit of giving in to the inertia that refuses to let us get up in the morning. These habits must be broken, but they never will till we make a basic commitment to a life of holiness without exceptions.*"[38]

That sounds good. He follows that up with, "*I found it difficult to say, 'Yes Lord, from here on I will make it my aim not to sin.' I realized God was calling me that day to a deeper level of commitment to holiness than I had previously been willing to make.*"[39]

Bridges is focusing on what the Christian is *not to do*, and while that appears to be a worthwhile pursuit, Christ seems to emphasize what the Christian *should be doing*, in His power, for this purpose.

---

[38] Jerry Bridges *The Pursuit of Holiness* (Navigator Press 2006), 92
[39] Ibid, 93

At one point, Bridges quotes from John Owen, puritan preacher who stated, "*Resolved, never to do anything which I would be afraid to do if it were the last hour of my life.*"[40]

Wrong Emphasis?

These are all good and valuable things that Christians should seek to accomplish, but I cannot help but wonder if the emphasis is wrong. If we spend our time understanding what God's love is (from *God's* perspective), and endeavoring to live a life of *love* (God's love, not what we may think love is), then will we not *automatically* be living a life of holiness? I believe we will.

Instead of intoning "*Resolved, never to do anything which I would be afraid to do if it were the last hour of my life,*" we would then be stating, "*Resolved, to live God's love to the very last hour of my life.*"

I believe that as soon as we start with the "*I won'ts,*" Satan is there with the "*Wanna bets?*" Just like New Year's resolutions, they do not last. If our focus is on what we should *not do*, however pragmatic, holy, or loving it may *appear* to be, we are still focusing on *ourselves*. If however, we focus on how to *love God and others*, we naturally take our eyes off ourselves and put them exactly where they belong.

I believe that becoming holy (practically speaking) is not accomplished by focusing on the way in which we are *not* holy. It is not by seeing how far short we fall that makes us holy. What makes us holy is the pursuit of living a life of love in full submission to God. It is in our union *with* communion with Him. Holiness is not achieved by determining how many things in my life need to be corrected, being fixated, and focused on *them* rather than *Him*. Turning our attention to Him alone will draw us into holiness. No list of "I won'ts" will ever get us there on our own strength. It is realizing how much more I need to *love* (God's definition of love, not the world's).

---

[40] Jerry Bridges *The Pursuit of Holiness* (Navigator Press 2006), 93

True holiness is, I believe, a *byproduct* of loving as God loves. It is not me focusing on my *shortcomings*, or what I need to get *rid* of that creates within me a sense of holiness. Holiness is not a feeling that can be measured. It is our *standing* that can be *seen in our daily life*. However, as soon as I start to see what I *perceive* to be my holiness, then that proves that I am *not* holy, because that is pride, which is sin. Just as Moses was unable to see his own face and the glow that emanated from it after meeting with God, we should also not see or be able to realize just how "holy" we are, because when we do, we immediately focus on SELF.

If I spend my time loving as God loves, in submitting to Him and His will, then the natural byproduct of that is becoming *holy*. Yes, Paul and other writers of the New Testament tell us to be *holy*, yet they do not say to chase after or pursue holiness. They simply say to *be holy*. To be holy is to love as God loves.

Examples of God's love, evidenced in a selfless and saving manner:

- Sent His beloved Son
- Granted us entrance to His family
- Showered us with blessings

Misery Loves Company

Show me a Christian who is chasing after holiness and I will show you an unsatisfied, miserable, judgmental person, who does not believe they can do enough to eradicate what they consider to be the *ungodliness* within them, or they have not completed the formula of prayers and actions that will result in greater holiness. Show me a Christian who loves more and more each day as God loves, and I will show you a Christian who is filled with joy because his eyes are not on himself, but on Christ!

Holiness is a byproduct of *loving as God loves*. In this way, holiness cannot help but be created within us. Holiness is not a feeling, though in many circles today, holiness has *become a feeling,* which compels us to *not do things,* or to do certain rituals that are supposed to produce holiness. This is not the way to holiness and in fact, I believe it is an extremely insidious form of self-righteousness born of *pride.*

Jesus never chased holiness! He *was* holy! Why? Because He only *did* the things (notice *positive* action), He saw the Father doing! Can you imagine someone being trained on a new job on his or her first day? What if the supervisor took them around and showed them everything that they were *not* supposed to do?

"Bob, don't ever do this as part of your job, all right?" says the supervisor. *"You are also never to go into this room, or touch that piece of equipment. None of this is part of your job, do you understand?"* asks your supervisor.

"Uh..right. Don't touch that, don't go in that room, and don't touch that piece of equipment. Got it!" you say.

"Excellent. You'll have this down in no time," responds your supervisor.

As the morning wears on, your supervisor continues to tell you all the things that are *not* related to your job and you have made copious notes, endeavoring to not do all that you are being told. You patiently wait for your supervisor to shift gears and start telling you what you *are to do,* but that never comes.

Finally, it appears as though the training is over. Your supervisor looks at you, then your notes, then back to you with a smile. *"Excellent,"* he states. *"You have made some great notes. I believe you will do a wonderful job, Bob. Any questions?"*

You look at him, attempting to hide your incredulity, and meekly say, *"Uh...well...you've outlined for me what I not supposed to do. I'm wondering though, exactly what am I supposed to do?"*

Your supervisor looks at you as if you are a complete moron. *"What do you mean what are you supposed to do? You're supposed to do everything else that is not part of what you are not supposed to do!"*

Obviously, the above scenario is absurd, but makes a point. No supervisor would train a new employee only to tell them what they are not supposed to do. In fact, by training them in only what they *are* to do, they will automatically know what they are *not supposed to do*. These two go hand in hand, but not the other way around.

Anyone who has ever been trained in any job is normally trained by being coupled with a person who already *does* that job. They can teach a new person that job by *showing* and *modeling* for them how it is done. During the process, they might also include a few "not to dos," but in general, they point out what **should be done** to complete the job responsibly.

Learning By Doing
I recall when I worked at a manufacturing plant back east for a few years. During my time there, I fulfilled a number of job responsibilities including quality control, or QC. This involved measuring the amount of metal thickness on substrates before they could move onto the next phase of production. Substrates with two little metal on them would not work well, and therefore would create an inferior product. The right amount of metallic surface was to exist before the substrates would pass inspection. We normally measured this by taking a few substrates from each section, and determining their measurements with acid, a different acid for each metal. Since there were three metals on each substrate, three different acids or chemicals were needed to complete the testing.

Job training happens when people are taught how to DO their job. Built into this method is the knowledge of what NOT to do in order to successfully complete the requirements that are connected to any job.

© 2010 F. DERUVO

During the process, in order for the substrate to pass inspection, the level of metal needed to fall within a specific range. Going below that range meant the substrate and that section needed to be stripped and the production process needed to start over for that batch. As long as each metal was within the range, everything was fine.

In reality, no one trains on a job by only being told what *not* to do. The bulk of the training covers all the aspects of what the trainee is supposed to *do* to ensure that the job is done correctly. By training someone how *not* to do a job, it will turn out that they will not have been correctly trained on how to actually *perform* their job function. They will only know what *not* to do, but will not understand *what* to do. We are to model what Christ did in His life.

It is impossible to look to Christ, while we are constantly dealing with things in our life that we believe we should not be doing. How can we do both things? We cannot do both things. Either we will be focusing solely on the things, which are wrong in our life, or we will be focusing on Jesus and how He lived, in an attempt to *emulate* Him.

Emulating Jesus
I believe that this was Jesus to the nth degree. He truly loved people and was concerned about their welfare, both physically and spiritually. He knew people were sick (from the sin nature) and He came not to condemn, but to give life. He spent hours at a time healing the sick, feeding the hungry, and preaching to the spiritually thirsty. He came to meet people's needs and He did so by not caring about His own.

Luke 10
In the gospel of Luke, chapter ten, Jesus tells us how we are to live, if we are authentic believers. If we are not authentic believers, then doing what Jesus says here will simply be *work* and *self-effort*, resulting in fatigue listlessness and a sense of wasted energy.

"The harvest truly is great, but the labourers are few: pray ye therefore the Lord of the harvest, that he would send forth labourers into his harvest," (Luke 10:2-3).

Jesus starts out by announcing the harvest is plentiful, meaning that there are many who *will* receive salvation. That is a guarantee. He also tells the 70 (He has just set aside for this purpose) that they should pray that more people would be raised up to help in the harvest.

"Carry neither purse, nor scrip, nor shoes: and salute no man by the way. And into whatsoever house ye enter, first say, Peace be to this house. And if the son of peace be there, your peace shall rest upon it: if not, it shall turn to you again," (Luke 10:4-6).

In order to do the above, a person has to trust Jesus to provide. That is a test of the character of the Christian. This is exactly what Jesus did. Once He left the carpenter's shop and stopped being a carpenter, He relied solely on God the Father to supply all His needs. The Father never failed Him and He will never fail us. Also note that by not carrying a purse, or money, or a suitcase ("nor shoes"), the reliance upon God becomes *real.* There are only two reasons to do this:

1. *Because we love God, and*
2. *Because we love people*

A person cannot be an authentic Christian without *authentically living* the life of a Christian in God's strength. That means imitating all that Jesus did.

While we do not have the power to heal physically, or to make a few loaves of bread and a few fishes multiply to feed thousands, we must do what we can do. If that means giving someone a pair of shoes, or buying them a meal, or preaching the gospel, then it must be done.

It is *impossible* to serve God and Self, and Satan has so many sneaky ways of making us believe that by focusing on our sins and failures, with an accompanying resolution to no longer do those sins and failures (even in Jesus strength), we are *still resolutely focusing* on our Self life, not His life in us and through us.

After the 70 returned, they rejoiced because even the devils were subject to them. Jesus warned that they should focus not on that, but that their names were written in the book of life (cf. Luke 10:20). Even so, we read these words immediately after that, "*In that hour Jesus rejoiced in spirit, and said, I thank thee, O Father, Lord of heaven and earth, that thou hast hid these things from the wise and prudent, and hast revealed them unto babes: even so, Father; for so it seemed good in thy sight. All things are delivered to me of my Father: and no man knoweth who the Son is, but the Father; and who the Father is, but the Son, and he to whom the Son will reveal him,*" (Luke 10:21-22).

Jesus rejoiced in His Spirit because of these things, and immediately gave thanks to the Father.

The Eternal Question

Not long after this, we read, "*And, behold, a certain lawyer stood up, and **tempted** him, saying, Master, what shall I do to inherit eternal life?*" (Luke 10:25; emphasis added).

Notice the phrasing there? A lawyer stood up to deliberately *tempt* Jesus to say the wrong thing. He wanted to catch Jesus in a faux pas that would have discredited Him in front of the people.

Instead of responding directly, we read, "*He said unto him, What is written in the law? how readest thou?*" (Luke 10:26).

The lawyer took the bait and responded with, "*Thou shalt love the Lord thy God with all thy heart, and with all thy soul, and with all thy strength, and with all thy mind; and thy neighbour as thyself,*" (Luke 10:27).

The lawyer gave the correct answer, and Jesus attested to that fact (cf. 10:28), but he immediately wanted to qualify it, as we see in the next verse. *"But he, willing to justify himself, said unto Jesus, And who is my neighbour?"* (Luke 10:29).

The lawyer wanted to find a way to sneak out from under the command to love *everyone*, so his question was *"who is my neighbor then?"*

At this point, instead of responding with a direct answer, Jesus tells the story of the Good Samaritan. Samaritans were considered "half-breeds" who were half-Jewish and half-Gentile. Since they were not authentic Jews, they were looked down upon by "righteous" Jews.

During the story, we learn that the only person who helped the man who had been robbed and beaten was the *Samaritan* (cf. Luke 10:30-36). Jesus ended the story with a question to the lawyer. Who was the one who actually loved his neighbor?

The lawyer had no choice but to respond with, *"He that shewed mercy on him,"* (Luke 10:37a). I'm not sure if the lawyer refused to use the word "Samaritan," or if it was simply more expedient to say it the way he said it, but the result is the same, with Jesus telling him to *"go and do likewise,"* (Luke 10:37b).

During the course of that story about the Good Samaritan, we learn what *not* to do:

- *Lie in wait to beat someone up and rob them*
- *Walk by without helping someone who needs our help*

Certainly, these two things are important for us *not do.* However, we also learn what we are *to do*, and in fact, that is the true emphasis of the story, or what is considered the *moral of the story*. We are to help those who need our help. That is how we love others and in doing so, we love God.

What do people need? They ultimately need *salvation*, so we must take the Great Commission seriously. If we love God and our "neighbor," we will evangelize the lost (our neighbor). We must also actively look for ways (not merely be *willing to do something*), to help those in need. Do we know people who need some furniture, food, help cleaning their homes, or people who are lonely and need visitation? These things are ways we show our love to them and to God and they often become open doors to sharing the gospel of Jesus Christ.

I firmly believe that this is *not* possible to do any of these things if we are energized by focusing on our faults and sin, especially if the doing of these works is done to earn holiness in the sight of God. If that is what motivates us, then we are in trouble, because we are not doing anything from a pure heart and that "energy" will not last. While it may *seem* as though our motives are pure, the actual motive has more to do with *us* than with the other person.

In other words, we see what we are *not* doing, so then we *force* ourselves to do what we know we *should* do. The better motivation, and certainly the more altruistic motivation is to do for others because of a deep sense of loving God and therefore, loving others.

Seeing Only the Right Way to Live!
It is fixing our eyes on Him that move *toward* Him and *away* from all that keeps us bound to this earth and this life. While many Christians prefer wallowing in how bad their sin makes them feel, God expects us to *realize* our sin, *confess* it sincerely, *believe* that He applies His forgiveness to that sin, and *move* on, continuing to *walk* more closely to Christ.

If we are to focus our gaze (actually to *fix it*), on Jesus, we will *only* see the right way to live. We will *never see* the wrong way to live. If we, by His strength, seek to imitate Christ, then we will by nature, be doing *only* those things that are acceptable to God. The emphasis is completely different from focusing on ME, and what I am doing *wrong*.

How is it possible to look to Jesus, while focusing on ME? Peter automatically saw how "dirty" and sinful he was when coming face to face with the holiness of Christ (cf. Luke 5:8). In other words, as we see Jesus, we *will* recognize our failures and our sin. As we continue to look to Jesus and submit our lives to Him, we *will* bring our lives in union with Jesus' so that our lives more and more mirror the life of Christ. We are not doing this by our own effort, because the Spirit of God resides within us.

Jesus said, "*Follow Me*" and He would make us fishers of men. He did not say, "*Follow Me, and I will help you focus on how dirty you are so that your time is used in purifying yourself through holiness.*"

We are to be holy in life as we are *now* holy in the spiritual realm. This comes from looking *to* Jesus, focusing *on* Jesus, and *imitating* Jesus. It is through this process that holiness comes to the fore and it comes to the fore without us even noticing it, because if we *do* notice it, then it is *not* holiness, but merely self-aggrandizement.

In Hebrews 4, the writer speaks of entering into a *rest*. This means we cease to work. Certainly, the writer is referring to the idea that some believe we must work for salvation. I believe the writer of Hebrews is also referring to the fact that by *working* in our own strength, we cannot make ourselves one bit holy (cf. Hebrews 4:10).

Insidious Nature of Pride

Pride in being "holy," pride in keeping self "holy," pride in finding the magic formula of rituals that will *lead* to holiness causes us to focus on what *we* can do. In point of fact, true holiness comes from a perfect submission to God, allowing His love to be made perfect in our weakness. This happens when we realize our utter dependency upon Him. This love then, reaches out toward the lost, and especially those of the household of God.

Though Satan prefers we keep our eyes on ourselves, let us turn our eyes on Jesus, the Author and Perfecter of our faith.

Resources for Further Study

INTERNET:

- Anti-Preterist Blog   antipreterist.wordpress.com
- Ariel Ministries   www.ariel.org
- Berean Watchmen   www.bereanwatchmen.com
- Foothill Bible Church   www.foothill-bible.org
- Friends of Israel   www.foi.org
- Grace to You   www.gty.org
- Loftus-Delusion   www.loftus-delusion.com
- Prophezine   www.prophezine.com
- Prophecy in the News   www.prophecyinthenews.com
- Study-Grow-Know   www.studygrowknow.com
- Study-Grow-Know Blog   www.modres.wordpress.com
- Tyndale Theological Seminary   www.tyndale.edu

Find more of Fred DeRuvo's books at the following places:

- Prophecy in the News   www.prophecyinthenews.com
- Study-Grow-Know   www.studygrowknow.com
- Amazon   www.amazon.com
- CreateSpace   www.createspace.com

NOTES

www.ingramcontent.com/pod-product-compliance
Lightning Source LLC
LaVergne TN
LVHW081353060426
835510LV00013B/1798